Peter Sinclair

A pIeCe Of DaDdY's HeArT

Titles by Peter Sinclair

♥

Memories, Thoughts & Photographs

Seasons of Success

A pIeCe Of DaDdY's HeArT

Peter Sinclair

A pIeCe Of DaDdY's HeArT

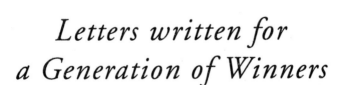

*Letters written for
a Generation of Winners*

THE CATALYST GROUP OF COMPANIES

National Library of Australia
Card Number and ISBN 0 9587188 3 0

Published by CATALYST BOOKS LTD
13 NEW ROW
COVENT GARDEN
LONDON
WC2N 4LF

E-mail:
sales@catalyst-group.com
Visit our website on: www.catalystbooks.com

Manuscripts are always welcomed from prospective authors
of motivational/inspirational material.
Please request a Submissions Guideline from the Editor.

Printed in Great Britain by
Redwood Books, Trowbridge, Wiltshire

This book is
dedicated to
the teachers of our
next Generation
of Winners

♥

- Mums and Dads -

*Such letters as are written from
wise men are of all the words of man,
in my judgment, the best,
for they are more natural than
orations and public speeches,
and more advised than conferences
or present speeches.*

– Francis Bacon

Contents

A pIeCe BeFoRe ThE mAiN pIeCe …

My youngest daughter cuddled up to me as I sat in front of the computer screen and she asked, *'How many more books are you going to write Daddy?'* I knew that behind her heavy sigh and her longing look she really wanted me to drop what I was doing and play with her. Although I have set many goals before, I found her question to be a tough one to answer. I leant over, kissed her little cheek, and wrapped my arms around her while I found just the right spot to tickle. With a scream of delight, she ran out of the room with me in hot pursuit. Amidst the raucous I thought to myself, *'I suppose that as long as my heart's in it there' ll always be another book.'*

Every time I read a book my mind searches for the passion of the writer. The heart of a writer, rather than his or her skill, is what inspires me. The books that grab me by the heart are the ones that make all the difference to my life. Although information is of vital importance, what I also need is the inspiration that will stir me into motion. It only takes one spark of inspiration to ignite an inferno of action.

The written word is so powerful that it can literally change your life. Within a whole library, it may only take a single book to make the difference. Within a whole book, there may be just one sentence. Within that one sentence, there could be a single word or phrase that will launch you from where you are to where you can be in the future.

The written word had a major impact on my life at the age of twelve, but rather than coming in the form of a book it came in the form of a letter. It changed my life. The contents of the letter are long forgotten but the associated emotions, as I read it, remain. I felt very special and very important because someone, whom I hardly knew, took the time to write to me.

What made that personal letter so special? I suppose it's because I was reading a piece of someone's heart.

The book that you are now holding in your hands is just that: a piece of my heart and I just happen to be a daddy or as my children get older, it's just plain dad. Deep down though I will always be a daddy. As you hold my heart in your hands, you are going to discover something. I am not only having a heart to heart chat to my children about how to live a successful life, but in fact I am depositing something very special into your own heart. As a parent and as a writer, my greatest desire for you who read my book is that you live life to the fullest in *health, happiness and prosperity*.

I don't mind if you take a piece of my heart and make it your own. There is a wonderful thing about hearts, in that there is always more than enough to go around. May a little spark from the pages of this book ignite within you a desire to experience the *'best of the best'* of what life has to offer you.

A suggestion from the Author :

These letters were written for the intent purpose of helping my children to gain yet another glimpse of the true meaning of success. Why don't you take some time out, from your own personal reading schedule, and sit at the end of one your children's or grandchildren's bed one night with this book in your hand. Read from it one of your favourite stories. Remember, a book shared can mean a heart repaired. Don't forget to read with expression and put on some of those funny voices from time to time. You know, the one's that make everybody laugh. Have fun!!!

If you have ever written a special letter to a child or a grandchild or have an inspirational story to tell, why don't you send me a copy. I want to gather many pieces of wisdom from many hearts, from all around the world, so that we can share them with others in future publications.

♥

Send your material to:

The Editor
Outasight Enterprises
P.O. Box 1218
MUDGEERABA QLD 4213
AUSTRALIA

Please enclose a self addressed stamped envelope
E-mail: editor@outasightenterprises.com
Visit our Website: www.outasightenterprises.com

THE 1ST LETTER

ThE pOwEr Of ChOiCe

A cold wind blew across the river and with every fresh blast it cut like a sharpened knife through her overcoat as she walked towards the bridge. In each arm she held a newborn baby; twins. Tonight, she had finally cracked under the strain that had been placed on her as she contended with a husband who failed to show her sufficient support and affection. To top it off she had suffered under the judgmental criticism of her husband's parents. With one child already, a girl, and now twins, her life was a pressure pot and she had suddenly lost all hope for a better life.

So with a baby in each arm she climbed up onto the bridge and prepared to jump. Through the mist, she could barely see more than a few feet from where she stood. However, as she prepared herself to plunge both her and her children into the dark depths of the cold river, she suddenly thought, *'No, I can't. I can't leave my daughter. I can't leave her!'*

That one thought saved their lives and the lives of the generations to follow as she climbed down from the bridge and returned home. The year was 1932.

♥

Children, the mother was your great grandmother and one of the twins was your grandfather. The choice she made that day has had far reaching implications for all of us.

What if she had jumped? You would have never read this book. Both of the twin's families would never have existed. Your great grandmother wouldn't have given birth to another three children and those families, with all their potential, would never have been born. A whole line of heritage would have been lost in a split second of choice.

It is so easy, in the rush of our daily lives, to underestimate the power of the choices that we make. As a child, I remember the choices that were the hardest to make: whether to have a chocolate paddle pop or a caramel one, whether to watch one cartoon on the television in preference to another, whether to play hand ball on the cement expanse at school or whether to play soccer down the back of the school toilets on the grassed area, whether to play with a friend after school or whether to stay at home and play with my dog. All choices, each and every one of them good but how does one really know if he or she is making the best choices in life?

It is well documented that there was a time in human history when the nation of Israel was given the choice between life and death. The wise advice given was that they would be better off if their choice was life. The incredible outcome is that the vast majority of that nation went on to choose death in the ensuing years. Why is that so? We are all given the power to choose.

I am so pleased that your great grandmother made a wise choice on that cold and misty night. I am alive because of that wise choice. I can breathe. I can feel. I can dream. I can write. I can express myself. I can kiss your foreheads every night before you go to sleep. I can sing to you in the morning, *'Rise and shine'*. I can run and hold you tightly in my arms.

She chose life that night when everything in her said that her best choice was death. Nothing made any sense to her. The pressures were too great and the responsibilities too high for her to see beyond her situation. She was smothered by circumstances. She couldn't breathe, she was blind, she was deaf, and she was lame, although to look at her she had no disability. She was crippled on the inside, right up until the point where she suddenly realized that she had a reason to live. There was a purpose greater than her feelings of helplessness. This purpose drew her away from destruction and brought her back to the point where she chose life. No matter how bad her life may have appeared at that moment it was a whole lot better than what death had to offer her and her children.

A lack of purpose and a lack of vision will destroy you. It will suck the very life out of your being. It is the stuff of losers and I see it in the eyes of so many as I walk through the streets of our nation. Deadmen and deadwomen walking but with no life in their eyes. There is no spark because there is no dream.

To live a life that is full to the brim and overflowing you must have a greater purpose. You must be the holder of a dream. You must grasp a vision that will drive you out of bed every morning. It will keep you motivated late into the night. When you clock off from work, you will be ready to get started on your driving ambition. It will fill you with joy as you work to see its fulfilment. A dreamer never looks at the clock. The dreamer doesn't have the time to look. They hone their skills so that they are better prepared to fulfil their dream. While everyone is off on the weekends, waiting for Mondayitis to kick in, they are learning how to get better at what they do. They have their eyes in the books that can teach them to get even more out of life and their ears are hooked up to the tapes that will supply them with both the inspiration and the motivation to press on with their dream. They are attending seminars: always willing to learn more and never afraid of making a mistake. In fact, they probably make more mistakes than the other ninety per cent who are too fearful to try. Although the dreamer is battered and bruised they have a smile on their face while they say, *'I've just learnt how not to do something.'* The winner chooses to do the best, to be the best and to seek what's best. The choices you make will determine the future of generations to come.

♥

As the operator pressed the button to lower the bridge, he heard a spinechilling scream come from below.

He had worked at the same job for years and years. He was responsible for the opening and shutting of the bridge that allowed the ships to pass through. These ships then made their way to the wharves to unload their precious cargo. It was a busy port and he was not only responsible for the safe passage of ships. He had to ensure that the passenger trains, that regularly crossed the bridge, reached their destination safe and sound.

His young son would constantly badger him to take him to work and the day finally came when he relented. His wife packed two lunches and sent both father and son off into the brisk morning air. She smiled as she watched them walk down the road, hand in hand. The little boy skipped while his father whistled a favourite tune.

It was like any other day: busy. Finding himself totally engrossed in his work he soon forgot that his son was playing at his feet. He also failed to notice that at some point during the day his son had slipped out of the control room.

Having just raised the bridge to let a ship through, he was suddenly alerted that a train was heading in his direction, ahead of schedule. It happened at times. Someone in the timetabling office would occasionally make a slight error of judgement, but there was usually sufficient time to correct it whilst maintaining a smoothness of operations.

That was when he heard the scream. He leant over to see out of the window of the control room's compartment, desperately trying to discover where it was coming from. He could just make out the outline of a small boy. He gasped, for it was his son. His leg was jammed in one of the mechanisms that opened and closed the bridge.

The bridge had already begun to close and the train full of passengers, returning home from a day's work, was speeding towards it. If he stopped the bridge from closing and left his post in order to free his son, the train would be derailed and all the passengers would either be killed or fatally injured. If he allowed the bridge to continue it's downward path his son would be crushed.

His brow suddenly flooded with beads of sweat as he was forced to make a choice. In that split second a battle waged within his father's heart. Who would he favour, his only child or the hundreds in the train?

Tears streamed down his face as he watched the carriage full of young schoolchildren, some as young as his son, waving and giggling as they passed safely over the bridge. Little did they realize that the deafening roar of the train was drowning out a sound that was breaking this man's heart into a million pieces.

The power of choice is in each and every one of our hands.

Choose well
Love from your Dad

*The winner chooses
to do the best,
to be the best
and to seek
what's best.*

THE 2ND LETTER

ReMeMbEr
NuMbEr ThReE

Children, there is something powerful found in the number three. A cord that is made of three individual cords is much harder to break than that which consists of only two.

So why is three such a powerful number?

There was once a man who found himself all alone. He didn't have a son and he didn't have a brother. There was never an end to his work. He was never satisfied. He would often ask himself as to whom he was working up a sweat for, because he seemed to be missing any enjoyment that life had to offer him. He was miserable because he was doing everything alone.

Two are always better than one because there is a far greater chance of a better return on their work. If one happens to fall down he has a friend who can help to pick him up. The one though who works on his own will be in great trouble if he happens to fall down because there will be no one to pick him up.

It is quite possible that one will be easily overpowered when under attack, two will more than likely be able to defend themselves but a three stranded cord will not be easily broken.

♥

A prisoner went to all sorts of trouble to escape from prison. Both he and his accomplices burrowed a tunnel that started at one of the cells. They continued to dig under the main wall until they had travelled quite a reasonable distance away from the prison compound.

Nearby the prison, there happened to be a preschool and it was while the children were playing in the playground that the prisoner lost all control. Although they had decided to make their getaway in the dark hours of the night, he couldn't resist the temptation to break out in broad daylight. It had taken them months and months of painful preparation to get to this stage but with a final push and with his arms raised high, he burst forth crying, *'I'm free, I'm free, I'm free!'* To his utter surprise, he found himself face to face with a young child. The prisoner, by this time was quite a sight with tufts of grass sticking from his mouth, his ears and a covering of dirt all over his face. However, the stern faced child, with arms on hips, took one look at the prisoner and confidently responded, *'So what, I'm four.'*

♥

There are **three qualities** that I wish to share with you. When entwined in your lives they will form a solid cord that will not be easily broken.

The first quality is **intelligence**. Now, when I write that word I am not thinking of your Intelligence Quotient (IQ) nor am I thinking of where you were placed in your last school exams. They are not even in my deepest thoughts, because I have seen many an 'intelligent' person who has been the star of the educational scene as we know it, top of the class, but who in life has become a total failure. The intelligence I am going to present to you goes far beyond the world of academia because the greatest lessons of life are learnt long before and after our institutional education.

When I speak of intelligence, I am speaking of wisdom and of understanding. I am speaking of 'life's' school; where you learn how to relate to others and how to walk in integrity in all your affairs. It is not in simply knowing your times tables, though that is a good thing. It is knowing how to budget your personal finances and to handle your affairs so that you can begin to turn all that you do into profit, whether it be for your own personal use or for the benefit of mankind. It is having the ability to think on your own accord, to make quality decisions and to take your own life into your own hands and to forge out a future that is productive and fruitful.

It is understanding what you have been given in life and knowing that it is your mature responsibility to build it and expand it through further study. To be intelligent is to recognize that we live in a world of ever-increasing change. We need to be pliable and flexible enough to take on board those things that are changing around us. We need to be humble enough to sit at the feet of leaders in their own respective fields and to learn and keep abreast of the facts.

An intelligent person is one who may not necessarily know everything but will know where to find the necessary information whenever it is required. An intelligent person surrounds him or herself with people who in many ways may be much smarter than themselves. They associate with those who are leaders in their own field. They avoid 'comfortable' by placing themselves in a position where their brain is forced to learn new things and where they are required to stretch their mind. They run to the uncomfortable and not away from it. They rush towards necessary change and never allow themselves to be cocooned in a changeless state. An intelligent person is one who has not only learnt how to work hard but has searched and found ways to work smart, by applying or implementing a system which will allow them to leverage their time. That truly is an intelligent person.

The second quality is **attitude**. In one of my other books I have mentioned that attitude not only determines altitude but also your latitude; this is your relationship with those you meet on a daily basis. It is the way you wake up in the morning that will determine the whole setting in a household. Happy people can make all the difference to the type of day their children will have at school and how their partner will react to clients in the ensuing hours. The whole tone of the morning will have a powerful impact upon all the lives touched in one day.

An attitude of gratitude will transform every day. As one person once said, *'If you wake up, it's a good day.'* We have so much more to be thankful for. We can be thankful for the sun that shines through our window in the morning, thankful for the rain as it refreshes the earth and rejuvenates everything that it touches; thankful for the birds that twitter in the cool breeze as it caresses the warm day; thankful for the air we breathe and for the laughter and even for the tears; thankful for the friends and for the family; thankful for the use of our faculties and for the fact that we have yet another day to live and share with others; thankful for another opportunity to bring joy into someone else's lives; thankful for the gift of writing as we send a note of encouragement to someone who needs to know that they are loved; thankful for the telephone and computer that allows instant communication for an encouraging word or thought to be sent to another. The greatest gift is to have an attitude that gives with no thought of receiving anything in return.

The third strand that makes this cord strong and unbreakable is **enthusiasm**. I suppose this is one of the qualities I admire so much in you my children. Your effervescent enthusiasm bubbles over me so often. As you burst through the door after a day at school or from a run in the park or even a swim in the pool, I am captivated by your joy and the unspeakable gift of life that you bring to my own life. As an adult, it is so easy to lose the spark and to become tied up in knots with the concerns of the day. It is like cooking a cake without self-raising flour, or porridge without a pinch of salt. Without enthusiasm, your life will fail to rise and it will always leave a bad taste in your mouth. Enthusiasm is vital if you are to achieve your goals and reach your dreams.

How do I get this enthusiasm? I change the way I use my body. I change the way I speak. I find that when I close my fist and punch into the air and speak out positive affirmations in a commanding tone such as, *'I am a champion'* or *'Nothing is impossible to me'* ... all of a sudden my whole demeanour is changed. My posture is alert, my mind is awakened from its depressed sleep and I am suddenly transformed in spirit, soul and body because I have acted enthusiastically. The clouds of doubt and despair are suddenly cast aside. Nothing may have changed in my circumstances but yet I have changed and because of enthusiasm, my mind is open to receive fresh ideas and fresh inspiration to deal with whatever I am facing at the time.

The three cords that are not easily broken; intelligence, attitude and enthusiasm. Build them into the makeup of your life and be the champion that you were born to be.

You're the best
Love Dad

*Make your
goals big enough
to stretch you
but small enough
to achieve.*

THE 3RD LETTER

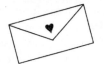

ThE aGoNy & tHe EcStAsY

My arrival at the foreign airport had been a harrowing experience. This was my first taste of a hostile situation. Armed guards, holding semi-automatic weapons, were stationed at every entrance. Stern faced, with no hint of emotion; they stood like statues guarding some sacred citadel. Trying to ignore the severity of the situation, I fumbled around in my luggage for my passport. This was to be one of a number of occasions that I had just missed a coup or an attempted coup in a third world nation.

Coming from such a peace loving and stable society I found it very difficult to adjust to nations that teetered on the brink of civil war. Those who inspected our bags were no more friendlier than those who guarded the terminal.

That was when my imagination took off on a rampage. I suddenly saw myself being roughly handled by some guards; each about six feet tall. They were dragging me down a dark alleyway that smelt dank and damp from years of seepage. We passed an area where chains and manacles were loosely suspended from the stone wall and I could just make out, in the dim light, that some of the rocks were smeared with the dried blood of the last victim. Further along the corridor I could hear a door being unlocked and a grinding sound as someone tried to pull it open. On arriving at the opened door, I was flung through the opening and landed headfirst onto a bed of damp straw. The door was slammed behind me. As I lifted my head, my eyes began to slowly adjust to the dim lit cell. I could make out a small barred window. As I turned, I was suddenly confronted by the hideous sight of the face of my toothless companion who had been rotting in this same prison for twenty years.

'Your passport sir!' I was suddenly plunged back into reality as I realized that the queue that I had been standing in for the past half-hour had suddenly moved on. It was now my turn to be inspected by the immigration officials.

It was more than an hour before I finally made it through to the passenger terminal and after spending so much time in the muggy environment my clothes began to swim in a lather of sweat. While recovering my luggage, it was wonderful to be met by the only friendly face in the terminal: my contact.

As I settled back into the seat of my friend's car, I sighed a huge sigh of relief. The threatening situation that I had found myself in, just minutes before, was now over and I looked forward to a hot bath and a light snack before retiring to bed. It had been a long flight.

Apart from the ever-present military presence in the streets and the long lines of people outside the bread shops each morning, my time in this strange country was without incident. I was even given free access to a vehicle so that I could explore the outskirts of the city while I was there.

My friend's house was set on an acre of well-manicured lawns and gardens surrounded by a tall and imposing wall. English in both construction and appearance, the brick building's second story was cement rendered and had been painted white. The roof was actually a combination of a number of smaller roofs. Obviously an architect's dream, where he had been given free license to experiment with his design. One of the entertaining rooms led out into an open courtyard paved with bush stone that flowed all the way around the pristine pool. The white outdoor furniture finished off the tranquil scene to perfection. Workers hired by the owners moved quietly throughout the house and the garden, as they maintained the property and kept it in good order. The peace experienced, as I sat beside the blue pool and sipped on a cool drink, was in stark contrast to what lay beyond the walls.

I had been in the country for only a few days when something happened that beckoned for a clear explanation. It came without warning and not even the owners of the house could explain what was about to happen. It was in the early morning hours, not long past midnight, when the whole household was awakened by the sound of single shots being fired from handguns, then there was machine gun fire and finally huge explosions as heavy artillery let loose their deadly weaponry.

I leapt to my feet and ran out of my bedroom into the hallway, thinking that my worst fears had been realized, and met the rest of the startled household. Was it an invasion? Was there a fresh ignition of the coup? Were our lives at risk? Would I ever get out of this country alive?

It was quite some time before the 'booming' and 'sharp cracking' sounds were silenced. By that time, we had all taken comfort in a freshly brewed cup of coffee. Our frantic discussion about the circumstances that had led to this outburst of explosions in the middle of the night gradually quietened as sleep began to overtake our eyelids. At least the threatening sounds hadn't encroached any further towards our home this night. One by one, we quietly returned to bed. The question though was, what would we find in the morning?

♥

Children, life has the habit of thrusting surprises in our path. These result in either agony or ecstasy: the agony of defeat or the ecstasy of victory. One cannot exist without the other. They stand hand in hand. They are two separate parts yet they make up the whole. It is what we learn in defeat that forms the strong foundations that will better equip us to taste the sweetness of victory. Defeat never means you are defeated, for it is not as important to win every skirmish as it is to win the whole battle.

Success is not a very good teacher. Your greatest teacher will be defeat and failure. With wisdom, you can look at each experience as a lesson to be learnt. Learn to identify the difference between what will bring you success and what will lead you to defeat again. Obviously, seek out success with all your heart, but never be dismayed if you fail to reach your goal first time around.

Take those big goals and cut them up into smaller portions. Make them big enough to stretch you but small enough to achieve. Achievement will continue to breathe into you the fresh sustenance that will carry you along for the whole journey.

If defeat has become your constant companion along the way, you may need to take some time out to find a wiser mind; one that has already walked the road you are presently travelling. Too many lives have climbed the ladder of what they perceived to be the ladder of success and have found themselves at the top of the wrong wall. If you are going to climb any ladder, it pays to check with the manufacturer and at least some of the other participants who have already climbed it.

Avoid defeat by getting the correct information. It's a smart way to live. Learn from the masters and you'll soon be taking firm control of your future as a master too. It will make you strong enough to buffet any attacks that come your way. You'll be ready for any surprises that life throws at you.

♥

We rose rather late the next morning because none of us had really welcomed the interruption to our sleep the previous night. By the time I arrived at the breakfast table, my hosts had listened to the radio broadcasts and had even purchased the latest copy of the morning newspaper. There was not even a whisper of what had occurred the previous night. Nevertheless, such was the way of this country. Things happened and were never reported. The media was often sworn to secrecy and only ever printed what the current government authorized. One would often have to wait until the message came through the 'grapevine', as it were.

By the end of that day, the buzz was that the leader of the country had suddenly decided to throw a celebratory party. He felt it was a significant date in the history of his country. He had mobilized the military, taken them into an open field, and ordered them to fire off their guns in the early hours of the morning. The only problem was that he hadn't alerted the general populous.

I suppose it was a bit like cracker night or Guy Fawkes Night with a slight twist. One thing I can say is that he caught our attention and he certainly won our admiration for originality.

The agony and the ecstasy …

Living life to the full
Love Dad

In helping others,
you will in fact
help yourself.

THE 4TH LETTER

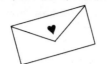

Be A pHoNy

'Be a phony? I thought I was supposed to be real?'

I recently commenced another business venture and in the course of setting it up, I decided that I needed to contact a selection of companies who were to be our competition. I wanted to find out their prices and to also see how professional they were. I chose the companies with the biggest ads in the yellow pages and also those whom I knew had been around for more than five years.

It was an amazing eye opener. I found that more than half of the companies failed; not on price, not on services provided, not on advertising artwork but in fact they failed in my eyes on the simple basis of the way their staff answered the telephone.

Some failed to give the name of their company. Others spoke roughly and gave you the impression that they really did not want to be there. Others tried to give you so much information over the telephone that you came away completely befuddled. There were even some organizations who had an answering machine turned on and the voice on the machine was droll, unenthusiastic and uninspirational.

There were a few though who answered in a clean and professional tone, supplying the facts when questioned and allowing the customer to make their own decision. There was no pressure, but one was given the impression that they were a professional company and that all their other services would follow at the same standard.

Now to this point you may think that I'm going to continue to report on what is negative about other people's telephone answering skills. That is not my point at all. My point is this. If you're going to operate a successful household or a successful business and supply a sense of joy and prosperity in your life, and in the lives with whom you communicate, then *you need to know how to speak on the phone.* Let's face it. We spend more and more of our lives holding this attachment to our ears and as far as I can presently see, this will be the way of the future, even with the introduction of e-mail and other forms of interactive communication.

In a sense, to be a phony is a true description of who I am at times when I answer the telephone. No matter how I feel, look or am dressed or undressed as it may be (I'll need to watch out for those phones that have television attachments) I need to, at all times, put on the voice that is going to impress the listener on the other end of the phone. I need to be the one who puts the spark into the conversation. It is so important that I develop the habit of 'being up' whenever answering the telephone.

What do you do when you don't feel like 'being up'? When it comes to business and you want the business doors to stay open, then you always need to 'be up' when you answer the telephone. But I am not just talking about business. I'm speaking of keeping families excited, keeping friends uplifted, injecting a sense of happiness, life and joy into the lives of the many strangers with whom you speak to during the day.

Even the carpet cleaning lady who is trying to sell you their service over the telephone. Treat her with respect and even though you may not buy her product, make it your mission to give her a great telephone call. She is the luckiest person alive because she rang you. Make her laugh. Help her smile, because the more you use this powerful communication tool to encourage others, you will soon find that others will start doing the same to you. It is a tough enough job canvassing over the telephone. They face a lot of rejection. So, even in your rejection you can accept her as a precious human being, worthy of respect and encouragement.

So children, how do you turn around any bad habits that you may have picked up along the way? Well here are a few tips which I have found helpful. Use them for thirty days with every telephone call and you will never approach the telephone again in the same manner.

1.	When you answer the telephone, make the decision, no matter how you feel, that you are going to answer it with enthusiasm. Put your body in a commanding position. Change your posture so that you stand upright. See yourself as a winner. I personally find that if I clench my fist and simply shout *'Yes'* I have immediately changed from a mouse into a man. By simply forcing my physical posture to change and by repositioning myself in that manner I have immediately changed how I see myself.

2.	You have now picked up the telephone and with an enthusiastic tone in your voice you have answered with your name, if you are at home receiving a personal call. You could say this, *'Good morning, Wally Walker speaking.'* If you are taking a business call then answer with both your name and the name of the company whom you represent. You could say, *'Good afternoon, This is Wally's Widgets, Wally Walker speaking'.* You have immediately identified yourself and established who you are and whom you represent. If you're feeling exceptionally jovial, when you receive a personal call, you may wish to answer, *'This is Sara Walker's fabulous dad'* or *'This is Julie Walker's macho man.'* The most important thing though is to speak in an 'up' tone of voice.

3.	When making business calls, it may help you if you jot down a few notes, either in your diary or on a notepad; both the purpose of your call and any pertinent questions that you wish to ask. It allows you to make an efficient telephone call and saves time. Those in business are generally very busy and they like to deal with those who appreciate the value of another's time.

4.   Purchase a telephone that will allow you to walk away from it while you're waiting to have your call answered. They have a loud speaker that projects what you normally hear in the earpiece throughout the room. This is particularly helpful when you ring those companies such as banks, airlines and insurance companies who have you wait on the line for quite some time. We are all familiar with the automated voice that says that they apologize for any inconvenience caused and that one of their operators will be there to answer our call as soon as possible. When they say 'soon', it rarely means soon at all. So rather than becoming 'fumed' you can be wandering around your office or house doing other more important things than hanging on the end of a telephone.

5.   Don't allow the telephone to rule your life. As the owner of a number of businesses, the number of calls that come my way can at times overwhelm me. This is where a secretary will be of assistance but if you don't have a secretary to screen your calls then it is alright, at times, to turn your telephone off so that you can concentrate on the tasks at hand. Being a writer, there are times when I need to be free of telephone calls. I would never get past the first page if I didn't manage them. You may choose to use some of the following: an answering machine, call diversion, messagebank, voicemail or paging service so that you can return the phone calls at a time that is convenient for you. The telephone is a tool for our lives and for our businesses. Don't allow it to become your master.

6.   Use e-mail, voicemail or facsimiles instead of making a telephone call. By jotting your thoughts down in this form, it allows you to clearly communicate your message. It will give the recipient of that message time to think about their response before getting back to you. I find this a useful habit when I need detailed information from my accountant, solicitor or business associate. It saves a lot of time hanging on the telephone for an answer.

7.   Never make an angry telephone call. Never send an angry e-mail, fax or any negative transmission. Maintain a positive attitude at all times when using this medium.

I heard of a funny experience where a client was a little upset about the way an executive was handling some details of their account. They decided to send their angry complaint to a friend via e-mail but as soon as they had pressed the send button they suddenly realized that they hadn't sent it to their friend but had in fact sent it to the executive with whom they were upset. I'm pleased to report that they are still friends and that they are still doing business together. Forgiveness is a good quality.

So whatever you do, go shout at the breeze or take a long stroll if you are angry, but never ever use these communication tools to express your anger.

8.   Finally, speak clearly and with a quickstep in your voice. I've said it before but it is worth repeating, put a smile on your face as you speak and have a sense of laughter in your voice. Know that apart from imparting and receiving information, you have again been given the opportunity to put something very positive into the life of someone else.

So children, be a real good phony. This is one time in your life when it's okay to be that way.

From one phonatic to another *Dad*

*A goal,
like a compass,
will guide you to
your planned
destination.*

THE 5TH LETTER

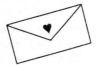

BiG aChIeVeRs PaY aTtEnTiOn To LiTtLe DeTaIlS

There were two men. Both had moved with their family to a beautiful spot beside a tranquil river. Both intended to build their dream home.

One of them was in a hurry to get underway and so failed to bother with a soil analysis, which would have revealed a soil with a very sandy consistency. He never consulted any engineers and failed to check any of the basic building details with any professional. He wanted a house and he wanted it now.

He had drawn up the plans in his spare time and because he was a naturally handy man he set about ordering all the materials required to build his new home. Within one week, he and a few hired labourers had the main construction up and the roof on. It wasn't going to be too long before both he and his family could move out of the local motel and into their new house.

Meanwhile, on the other side of the river, his friend had pitched a tent on the land he had purchased. It wasn't easy to pitch the tent because as they tried to bang the tent pegs into the ground they struck rock. In the end, after a dozen pegs were bent, they grabbed a few rocks and attached the ropes to them instead. He had taken the time to check with the local council about the specific building requirements, had his plans prepared by an architect, had the land checked and surveyed, hired a builder to assist him and was going to act as his labourer.

On the sandy side of the river, it wasn't too long before the final door was hinged and the last window inserted. The carpet was laid and the new family moved in. The owner walked out onto his front verandah the next morning and laughed as he looked across the river. He thought to himself that a snail must have been employed to build his friend's house. Only the foundations had been laid and what a racket they were making as they excavated into the rock beneath.

Life continued for both families. The one who had long completed his quick construction was out playing tennis and swimming in his newly installed pool. He was generally enjoying life while his friend on the other side of the river was working hard. Systematically, he was insuring that not one detail was overlooked as he assisted in the building of his dream home.

Quite often, his neighbour would pop in to have a chat; to see what progress was taking place. He was getting a bit bored and constantly badgered his friend to put down his tools and come out to play. The response was always the same. When he had completed the task of building his house properly, then and only then would he be ready to come and join in the fun.

Many months passed and the day finally arrived when the second family moved into their new home. It was a time of real celebration. At times, as he laboured alongside the builder, he wondered if he was ever going to finish his house. There had been many interruptions along the way because of unanticipated delays. Inclement weather had at times brought the building process to a standstill but yet the dream of having a solidly built home, overlooking the river, was what kept pushing him on.

His friend from across the river popped in with a bottle of champagne, because he was finally pleased that he could have someone to join him on his jetski, tennis court and on the golf course. It had been a lonely time these past months and he couldn't understand why his friend had built the house so tediously in this day and age of fast track methods.

The days soon passed into weeks and the weeks moved on into months as both families enjoyed their lifestyle by the banks of the swift flowing river: a little bit of fishing, a little swimming, some jet skiing and water skiing. It was generally a place where they could experience the joys of a holiday atmosphere three hundred and sixty five days a year, without ever leaving home.

But then the day came, when at ...

6.00 p.m. the skies opened up. Within a very short time, the cloudy sky had dumped more rain on this area in one night than was ever received in one season. The term buckets would have gravely understated the quantity of water that fell. That's when the man who built his house quickly on the sandy surface began to get worried. The river had started to rise at an alarming rate.

11.00 p.m. Other neighbours came to help after he had sent out a distress call. Even the local fire brigade was called in. It was all hands on deck as they began to fill bags with sand in order to keep the flood waters back. However, try as they may, the volume of water was starting to rise faster than they could fill sandbags. The scene was one of chaos. There was yelling and shouting, people running here and running there. They worked under the dazzling lights and to the sound of generators as they strained to pump and redirect the flow of the threatening water.

3.00 a.m. Even his friend, from across the river, had to finally leave and return to his own house because the bridge was being threatened.

6.00 a.m. As the dull light of a new day surfaced, it unveiled a scene of total devastation. Those who had been filling sandbags since the previous night were catching a few minutes sleep, while others were preparing and distributing both food and hot coffee to the workers. The rain was still teeming down but as he looked across the river, he could just make out the house that had been built on the rock. It too was still under threat but when talking to his friend on his mobile phone he discovered that the foundations, though awash with water, were still holding firm.

10.00 a.m. The walls broke on both sides of the bank. It happened just seconds apart and as the floodwaters rushed up against the house on the sandy ground, the workers were lucky to escape with their lives. For it came in with a rush, picked the house up from its flimsy foundations, and began to crush the complete structure as if it were made from matchsticks. The whole house was lifted up into what appeared to be arms of water and the dismantled structure began to be transported further down the river, broken up, piece by piece, along the way. This was a houseboat that wasn't going to last the distance. The man and his family held each other arm in arm as they watched their dream disappear before their very eyes.

Through the tears, they looked to the other side, the rocky side, and could see the water rushing all around the base of the other dream house. He thought to himself that it wouldn't be long before this house too, would follow the path of the one he had just lost.

12.00 noon. The rain stopped. The surging floodwaters began to slowly recede. All that was left for the workers to do was to start cleaning up the debris. A thick white mist settled all over the river after the rain stopped and no matter how hard one looked it was impossible to see the other side.

All communication lines were down and the battery of his mobile had run flat. Part of the bridge had collapsed and there was no way he could ever know of what had happened to his friend; the one who had built on the rocky surface. He was sure that their house, too, would be in ruins because the floodwaters had engulfed the lower story very quickly.

Suddenly a shaft of bright sunlight broke through the

clouds. As it increased in intensity, the mist was gently pushed aside. He could see his friend. He was waving from the second story balcony of his house, still secure, still solid … a little damp, battered and bruised but at least his dream home was still standing.

♥

Children, none of us can ever avoid the storms of life but we can prepare for them by paying attention to the details of our lives. Make certain that the foundations of your life are firmly built on solid rock principles rather than the shifting sands of popular thought. To be a leader and to be in for the long run will require you, from time to time, to stand against the opinion of the masses. You may have to swim against the current and stand up for what you believe in. You will need to work harder and smarter. You will need to invest your time into those things that will help you build a strong and secure future. You may fail, but you will be strong enough to get up again. You will have learnt from your mistakes and will have improved your life based on experience and acquired wisdom.

Go for it
Love Dad

*Remember,
always have a
tank full of
thankful.*

THE 6TH LETTER

AdD yOuR sIgNaTuRe

One of the proudest moments in my life was the day that I could write my own signature. I wrote it on a deposit slip as I deposited money into my new savings account. For hours and hours I would spend time practicing to develop my own personal signature. I would practice it when I wrote letters to my friends or relatives. I would practice it when I had to sign on before each soccer game. One of us would bend over while the rest of the team filled out the player's card with their individual signatures.

Other people's signatures used to fascinate me. Some of the girls in my class would put love hearts above their signatures, particularly when they passed love notes around the classroom in Year 6. I recall other girls putting a big circle above the letter 'i' rather than a dot. Some would scrawl while others were neat as neat. I could never understand my doctor's signature but I was always impressed with the ease that both my mother and father would write their signature on cheques or in letters that they had just written.

The first thing that people look at when you use your credit card or show your licence, is your signature. Your signature is you and you are your signature.

See children, it is all about being an individual and of being proud of your own individuality. You may ask, *'How do I achieve success and wealth in business?'* Try being a non conformist. Be an individualist. By doing so, you will be amazed at how fast you get ahead. Be you. Your originality, imagination, resourcefulness and self-reliance will assist you in achieving real lasting success and happiness.

You will be the fish swimming upstream while all the others are floating in the opposite direction. For that is the way of the masses and is definitely not the way of someone who has put their signature on everything that they put their hands to. You will be the optimist while the world grovels in its pessimism. You will be constantly looking for new and better ways to do and make things.

Watch an individual who is constructive in their individuality and see them rise head and shoulders above the crowd. They are the dreamers; the ones with new ideas and fresh insights. They are never satisfied to swallow what is acceptable but are willing to explore where no man has gone.

This is the person who has the capability of thinking and acting on their own and is unafraid of what others think or say; for this one is a non-conformist. This is the person who comes against a problem and rather than running from it will stop and search for a solution. In their mind, problems are opportunities for victory and even opportunities to make a profit.

They look at things that people may hate doing and decide to do it for those same people at a price. This is the source of their great wealth. They look at ways of working smarter than simply working harder. They look at a piece of dirt and see a glorious resort that will bring joy to thousands of families. They look for opportunity where others fail to see anything of value.

♥

I recall the story of a cleaner who was cleaning the foyer of a great skyscraper. A lady walked by with her son in hand. The child was throwing a tantrum at the time and she quickly pointed to the cleaner saying, '*If you don't start to behave you will end up just like him.*' With that statement, they left the building.

The cleaner overheard what the lady said and after he had finished washing the floor he put away his equipment, undressed and began to chuckle. He left the building to hop into his brand new Rolls Royce. He was in fact the owner of a multi-million dollar cleaning company that spanned the globe. He had just filled in this afternoon for one of his workers who had suddenly fallen ill.

♥

My motto:

'Do what others won't do and then you'll have what others will never have.'

The one who puts their signature on whatever they do will seize the opportunities around them. Their minds are always searching for ways to devise new products and new and more effective ways to get the same job done. They seek for a system that will allow them to do more with less effort. This will enable them to expend more energy into other ventures. They look to squeeze more production into the same hours that have been given to other men. They may rise early or they may stay up late in order to achieve even greater achievements. They have an eye for detail. They are leaders who receive input from the specialists that surround them, but at the end of the day they make the final decision. They give the necessary direction to those working with them and take full responsibility for the outcome. They are resourceful and aggressive and rely on their own abilities and judgments.

They enjoy the creative process and through their demonstrated ability and achievement, no matter how unusual their signature may be, those who appreciate the life of a winner will respect them.

Make a list of five businesses. Think of those who present a total package of excellence. What is their signature? What mark have they made on your life? How have they achieved that level of excellence? What sets them apart from the rest of the field? What is significant about their contribution to the world that we live in? Is there someone out there who you could begin to model yourself on? I know that as a child I would try to copy many and varied great people. It was like a footstep in the sand. I stretched to put my little feet into the impressions made by their feet until I finally had feet big enough to step further.

Children, as the years pass by you will face the pressure to conform to mediocrity. There will be those who will try to keep you from becoming what you were born for. For there is an element in our society who despises anyone who would step out of the crowd. Even friends and relatives may seek to hold you back from moving ahead. Not all will applaud you as you pursue something that has never been pursued by them. These though will be the very same people who will pat you on the back when you have finally achieved.

However, with or without the support of those, from whom you would have expected support, you need to add your signature to everything you do. Be an individual. Be radical. Be outrageous. Be dynamic. Be adventurous. Explore new worlds. Experiment with new ideas. Spread your wings like eagles and fly. Push ahead in the direction that you believe you should push. Dare to be different. Express your own originality in everything you do. Expect excellence and add a touch of class to everything you do. Go the extra mile. Look for something others have missed. Seek out better ways to serve, whether it be to a fellow staff member or a client. Be alert and always be on the lookout for something that will set you apart from the norm. Do something extra. Have fun with thinking of ways in which you can place your personal signature on whatever you do.

Here are a few suggestions that can help you to add that little touch of class.

♥ After completing a task for a client write a short thank you note, thanking them for their business.
♥ Leave a personal card

- ♥ Send a personal fax
- ♥ Write a personal e-mail
- ♥ Buy some flowers (I remember one Christmas when I decided that it would be nice to send a bunch of beautiful flowers to every one of the businesses that we had conducted business with throughout the previous year. The next day I had one of those business owners give me a call. She was crying happy tears. Not once, in all her years in business, had she ever received such a lovely gift from a customer.)
- ♥ Make a donation to someone's favourite charity or ministry on their behalf and tell them.
- ♥ Buy a small gift. (With one business we owned we would simply leave small Easter eggs in the clients homes at Easter time. The only challenge with this act was that when the parents came home, all that was left were the screwed up pieces of coloured foil that had once covered the Easter eggs. The children had found them before the parents came home from work. In future, we kept larger stocks in store so that the whole family could enjoy the treat.)
- ♥ Make a personal telephone call for no reason whatsoever.
- ♥ Send a gift out of the blue
- ♥ Send a birthday card

You can probably think of many other ways to creatively put your signature on whatever you do. Make it special and make it yours.

Signing off
Love Dad

Major on your strengths and delegate your weaknesses.

THE 7TH LETTER

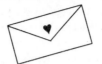

DeVeLoP a GoOd StUdY hAbIt

One of the greatest studies that you can ever make is the one that will unveil the secrets behind human lives. I make it my habit to study people. I see myself as a scientist who observes the lives of others under the microscope of my observations. Whenever I read a book or listen to a tape, I am seeking to unveil what makes the writer or speaker tick. I am looking for the secrets that they have discovered. I'm searching for what has given them the leverage in their life or the success that they have already achieved.

I also observe those who have not yet achieved. I ask myself what makes one person achieve, while another doesn't seem to be able to lift their chin above the mire of despair and hopelessness? What is it that separates human beings into different levels of success? Now I am not just speaking in monetary terms. I have written in my other books that I have slept in village huts with people I would consider as being rich, yet I have visited those in palatial settings whom I would have considered poor.

As I sit in a local mall and watch the people go by, I often ask myself, why is it that only 1% of them will ever be wealthy and at the most 5% will be in a healthy financial position by the time they are eligible to retire? Why is it that 95% of humanity will end up either dead, broke or disabled before they hit their twilight years? What is the common ingredient? Why don't more people grab hold of opportunity and run with it? Why are people satisfied with the status quo?

These are the very questions that drive me to pursue my own personal success and as Malcolm S. Forbes says, *'a vital ingredient of sustained success is occasional failure.'* A truer statement has never been spoken, because this is one of the major reasons that separates a winner from a loser. Losers fail and winners fail. It's not failing that makes the difference but it is the way that they deal with the failure. This is the defining line between success and failure.

Success is not a good teacher at all. In fact, it can breed a greater destruction of good habits than anything else can. It can make one lackadaisical and cause one to lose one's sharpness. Beware of success but at the same time strive for it. It is like a lion and you are the lion tamer. Success must be controlled and when a goal has been attained, it is important to have another one ready to reach for, so that you can begin to scale upwards to the next level of achievement.

To be a successful human one has to constantly live with a mission in mind; with a mountain to climb and a star to reach. This is what drives people on to greater achievements. This is what breathes life and excitement into every day that you breathe.

♥

Children, let me share this story with you.

There once lived a young boy who heard of a great man. It was said that this man knew of the many mysteries of life and nature that had been hidden from others. Therefore, the young boy made a decision. He would go and ask the man about the secret of his discoveries.

The man lived in the mountain areas, which meant that the young boy would have to walk all day before arriving at his destination. He would have to courageously overcome a whole range of obstacles before reaching the little hut that was owned by the wise man. It required the climbing of many hills and mountainous outcrops, the traversing of valleys and the crossing of a great river over a suspended bridge. He would also need to pass through a deep, dark wood. There were many stories told of those who had gone into the wood and had never returned. Unperturbed, he would go.

It was early one Saturday morning when he set off on his journey, long before the earth had struck its match to ignite the morning sun. His family was still asleep. The first they knew of his expedition was when they gathered around the breakfast table that morning and discovered his note. By the time they were made aware of his absence he was far away.

The journey became increasingly treacherous because instead of the sun lighting his path, the sky began to be filled with dark threatening clouds. The wind began to howl. The boy struggled to see where he was going as the wind whipped up the dust and sand and hurled it like thousands of sharpened darts against his face.

At one point, he pulled out the map from his knapsack, to check his bearings. Before he was able to open it, the wind caught it and flung it over the side of the hill he'd just climbed. Fortunately, he had been studying this map for a long time and had memorized it completely. He was so pleased that he had taken the time to do so because it was that knowledge that would be the source of his survival.

As he climbed higher and higher, he struggled against the force of the elements as they dumped their anger on him. Finally, he broke through the cloud cover and to his utmost surprise he burst into an area that was bathed in brilliant sunshine.

There before his eyes, was a little cottage nestled into the side of yet another mountain peak. Not more than one hundred metres from where the cottage stood, he saw a man sitting on a rock that overlooked the valley he had just climbed.

The boy approached him cautiously, wondering what he was going to find. In his village there had been many different stories told about the man who lived on the mountaintop. Some were good, some were bad, but amidst it all there was a mystery surrounding his life which had captured the imagination of the boy. As he tentatively approached the man from behind, the man suddenly turned.

The boy had expected a very old man, but to his surprise the man was young in face and gentle in features. He was not what he had expected at all. He was not weather beaten, nor gnarled by the harshness of the winter months.

The young man spoke to the boy, *'And what brings a young fellow like you up here to the mountains?'*

The boy stepped forward but found that although he had opened his mouth there was nothing forthcoming.

'Speak up boy, speak up,' urged the man with a note of urgency in his voice.

'I have come to see the man who knows the secrets of life and nature.'

'Why would you want to meet such a man?'

'Because I want to know of his secret.'

'Secret?'

'Ye-ss', there was an added stammer of excitement rising in the young boy's voice. *'I want to be wise like the one who lives here, but I thought you would be old.'*

'Well, what do the people in the village say about this man you speak of?'

'Oh, they say that his friends are the eagles who soar high above the peaks. They say that he speaks with the bears of the treacherous wood. They say he talks to the mountain goats as they move higher in the summer months to graze on the fresh grasses that have been hidden by the snow during the winter months. They say that he calls to the swallows and knows the seasons and the

times intimately. They say that he knows the ways of the wind and the mystery of the storms …'

'Hold on, hold on!' interrupted the man as he held his hand up in an effort to stop the flood of words coming out of the young boy's mouth. *'That all sounds very impressive, but what do you expect to gain from him?'*

That was a question the young boy had failed to really think about. His curiosity, more than anything else had brought him up here. *'Now that you ask, I suppose I want to know what you know.'*

'Me? But you don't even know me.'

'But you are the man whom they speak of in the village?'

'No, I'm sorry to disappoint you, but I'm not that man.'

The young boy paused, while giving the man a knowing glance. *'I thought you were a bit young. Well where is he?'*

'He is not here. I have come year after year to this place ever since I was a young boy like you and have never seen him. I have never met with him and never talked with him.'

'Then why do you continue to come?' asked the young boy.

'Because each year he leaves a message marked in one of these rocks, usually only one word in length. To read this message is why I return to the mountain. It sustains me throughout the following year and gives me fresh inspiration until I return.'

'What word has he left this time?'

'Here it is. I'm sitting on it.'

As the man moved off the rock, the young boy moved forward to see the one word that the wise man had left. However, as his eyes squinted in the sunlight, he turned to the man and said, *'But I can't see anything.'*

'Look closer.'

'There's nothing there, just a big old rock that's been here for thousands of years. Do you mean I have come all this way for a rock that doesn't even have a message on it and to see a wise man who doesn't even exist? What's the point? I may as well have stayed at the bottom of the mountain like everybody else.'

'But you didn't. That's what makes you different. Look at the rock again!' urged the young man. As he looked again, there to one side of the rock was the single word 'study'. It had been finely carved into a contoured section of the rock. *'I see it. It says study.'* The boy looked up from the rock and back at the young man asking, *'But study what?'*

'Ah, now that is the challenge. That is what you must go away and study. For through your questioning you will discover the answer. The longer you seek answers and look deeper beneath the surface, the more you will see and the more you will learn. Though you return to the valley you will always, from this day forward, have the spirit of the mountain within your heart. There is no time to waste. You have much to study.'

Study to be better
Love Dad

THE 8TH LETTER

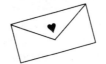

ImAgInE a NeEd AnD fIlL iT

Children, your imagination is a powerful tool that needs to be continually developed. When people ask me what I do, I have only one answer and that is; *'I am in the creation business.'* Even as I write this letter, I am typing these words, one letter at a time onto a blank page. I am creating something that has never existed before in the history of humanity. It's something worth shouting about because it is an original creation birthed out of my mind and my heart for you, the reader, right now.

Each of us, every single minute of the day, has the opportunity to create something that has never been created before. There is no limit to how our imaginations can assist us in this task.

Many think that the use of imagination is limited to those in the arts: to the composer of music, the designer of fashion, to the stroke of the artist and the writer of books. No, this is completely wrong. It is linked with every facet of life; from the cooking of a fine meal to the way you carry out the chores around the house, the way you write a letter to a friend or to the way you carry out your daily activities on the job. It is entwined in the way you design and carry out a business plan and even to the way you balance your chequebook.

Imagination is what helped humanity to move from the horse and cart era to the age of the automobile. Imagination took humanity to the moon and our technology to Mars. Imagination brought us the age of fast food restaurants. Imagination put electricity into our homes and helped Thomas Edison to create so many life improvement products. Imagination brings constant change into our lives at an ever-increasing rate. Imagination causes the product that I bought today to be outdated tomorrow.

How can we use our imagination to better our lives and the lives of those around us? As a child, we find that our imagination and the worlds that we create within our minds are mainly for our own personal benefit, except for the times when we choose to share it with a close friend. I have watched you, my children, as you have constructed mighty buildings and highways with building blocks. I have observed you with your imaginary tea parties and as you have entertained royalty and other officials. I have listened to your conversations between teddies and dolls. There have been other times when you have spoken strongly to an imagined friend or taken on the role of your mother and father. It was as if I was listening to my own self as you repeated phrases that I have spoken, or the instructions I have given.

With all the lights turned off in the house, you have gathered the family together for a performance. You have set up the portable tent and performed puppet plays through its open window in the torchlight. With your imagination you have brought stuffed animals alive and transformed the silence into a place of laughter. You have stunned the imagined audience with your presentation. You have overwhelmed us with your enthusiasm as you present your plays, sing your songs, and dance your dances.

That very same imagination should carry you through and onwards into adulthood. Turn your imagination onto a need and then seek out a way to fill it. By doing so, you are not only going to bring great blessing to yourself and your family but you will in fact bring great joy to many others.

That, I believe is why God created you with the capacity

to imagine. He being the ultimate creator and you being formed in His image, He has injected you with the same desire to create. So use this capacity, identify your own particular talents and then search for the need that you are going to fill. Imagine what changes you will bring to other people's lives, whether it is a product, a service or simply a kind act. Ask yourself, how can I create a special moment in another's life? The one who is always seeking out ways to add a positive dimension to other people's lives is always the winner. The giver is the gainer.

♥

I recall a children's story that I once read to you. It was about a little duckling that had fallen down a deep hole. Many people began to gather around to see what they could do to help this little duckling.

Some people threw food down the hole. Others offered many and varied suggestions to retrieve the forlorn little creature. Suddenly someone came up with the idea of filling the hole with water. One woman gasped, *'But it'll drown!'* However, as the humans organized themselves into a human chain that stretched from the hole to the nearest fountain, they began to pass water. They put water in whatever implements they had at hand. As more water was poured into the hole, the little duckling began to float higher and higher to the surface. When the water had finally reached the top, the little duckling waddled off with the rest of his brothers, sisters and mother, safe and sound. Now that is an example of how to use your imagination for good.

♥

As we turn to the daily news, whether it is in a newspaper, a magazine, or the radio or television, we are constantly reminded that we live in a world of great need. The key to your success is to identify a need, imagine it if you will and then seek out a way to fill that need to overflowing. It is the searchers who are the finders. It is the seekers who are the keepers. It is the investigators who are the discoverers. It is the risk takers who are the achievers. The ones who are willing to thrust out from the shores will be the finders of new lands and new civilizations. It is the dreamers who take us to places where we have never been.

So take a pen and paper and begin to design your fresh idea. Draw sketches, as crude as they may be and begin to let your imagination run riot. This is for you, not for anyone else. I trust that you have already started to keep a journal or a diary of your daily thoughts. One of the greatest tools for me, for fine tuning an idea or identifying a solution to a problem, has been my habit of keeping a journal. Some may choose to keep it in an exercise book. I in fact keep two. One in a book and the other on my computer. Both are valuable tools for the expansion of ideas.

Just the other day, as I discussed with a WebPage designer the features I needed for a couple of new WebPages, he asked me what I required. I was able to reach down into one of my journals and pull out the notes I had made many months before. The exact details were written for just that purpose.

Your journal is the incubator of your ideas and the recorder of your imaginative thoughts. If not recorded, they can pass through the air unnoticed and will never surface to bless both you and those around you.

Make it your habit to spend a little of each day to imagine. Take some time to record an idea and of course, some more time to put them into action. Each step will carry you closer to the fulfilment of your dreams. This is how your horizons will expand, and at the same time you will be filled with the joy of knowing that you have laid another building block in the foundation of your destiny.

To my children, who are beyond my wildest imagination ... pure joy.
Love Dad

THE 9TH LETTER

StIcK wItH yOuR sTrEnGtHs

The crowd gasped as we watched the small muscular frame of a man make a final attempt to lift the huge weights. They seemed to be as big as him. Well that's how we saw it as we sat up at the back of the stadium. The rest of the competition had faded away as he continued to push past limits that had been thought humanly impossible. Now he was to try for the ultimate prize so that he could once and for all stand on the podium as not only the winner of the competition, but in fact the world champion. He would be recognized as the world record holder of his category at this prestigious international event.

A hush came across the auditorium as he stepped up to rub some chalk dust on his hands. Sweat, even at this point was noticeable on his brow. His tanned muscles rippled as he rubbed his hands until they were completely white with the dust. His steely glance clearly exposed his complete focus on the task at hand. His sure step and his purposeful movements filled the crowd with more and more confidence. Some though gave way to a slight tinge of doubt as they thought, can this small framed man possibly break through the barrier that has never been conquered by another human being of his stature?

The competitor had visualized this scene in his mind day after day, month after month and year after year. He had pushed his body, stretched it, and strengthened it, all because after trying sport after sport, and never achieving, he had finally discovered the place where he could reach his dreams. Even though he was a failure as an athlete, even though he had not been accepted into the national football league and had been knocked out time and time again as a boxer, he had finally found the sport for which he had been specifically designed.

Little did the crowd know of the many painful hours he had spent in physio to be able to reach this event. Only months before the world competition he had been knocked from his pushbike one night as he rode home from training. He had sustained a stress fracture in his left leg and been bruised from head to toe. At that point, he made a decision. He would still pursue the goal and would not wait another four years to become world champion.

♥

Many had asked him what had driven him to the pinnacle of his chosen sport. He had responded, *'I didn't really care what I was to do, as long as I could do something and do it well.'* Excellence was his credo. He had demonstrated that same spirit in every single sport he had pursued. All his past coaches agreed that even if this man lacked certain skills in any given sport he tried, he never lacked enthusiasm. They also pointed out that he was never afraid to change direction when he recognized that his gift in a particular sport was not being realized. He was never afraid to start at the bottom again in another field and climb the ladder systematically. His aim was to always maintain a positive state of mind and a fit state of body. In doing this, he was able to flow freely between each sport until he finally found his mark. It took years for him to find his forte in sport, but he never regretted the lessons learnt along the way. Some of the most valuable lessons were learnt when he failed.

One of his earliest lessons came when he was only a child. He was the short, skinny kid in the class. He was the one that the bullies targeted for punching practice before, during and after school. They would call him 'matchsticks' because of his skinny legs; kick his school bag about and taunt him every day. Consequently he hated school and looked for any way to avoid it. This then brought him under the scrutiny of the teachers and if the bullies weren't beating him, he was being caned for truanting.

He was from a very poor neighbourhood and it was a struggle for his mother to keep food on the table. His father was always stealing the food money to buy himself and his mates another drink down at the pub. The harder she worked, by getting odd jobs such as cleaning, ironing and washing, to put some food on the table for her son, the harder it seemed to keep the money away from her husband. He only lived for the next drinking binge. Then there were the times when his father would come home late at night, wake up the whole household and start to break things and beat up his wife. The young boy would cuddle up to his pillow and huddle into the corner of his small room, afraid to go asleep, lest his dad would storm into his room and yell abuse at him.

It was during those times that he determined in his heart to never be like his dad. He would become something that both he and his family would be proud of; free of poverty and free from the bondage of a deprived past. It had been that background which had driven him from one achievement to another. It had enabled him to stumble over hurdles and to climb obstacles that would have stopped others in their tracks. It was this spirit of a champion that supplied the energy to get up and try again every time he had fallen. That same spirit had brought him to the podium this very night.

♥

By now, he was standing in front of the capacity crowd. They had all come to watch the one whom they still nicknamed 'matchsticks'. By this time in his career though, any derogatory names bounced off him like bullets deflected from a bulletproofed vest. It wasn't what others said to him on the outside that counted. It was what he knew in his heart that would carry him across the line.

The broken leg had healed up well, but by the time this final event was nearly over he could feel tiredness creeping up that same leg. It hadn't been there on the previous nights but ignoring it, he moved forward to where the weights were waiting to be conquered. He rubbed his hands together and with fixed concentration he bent over, grabbed the bar, and flexed his fingers at the same time, as weightlifters do. *'Relax, relax, relax',* were the words he quietly whispered to himself. The moment had come to complete the perfect 'clean and jerk'.

The silence in the auditorium was thick with tension. Before anyone could take another breath, he pulled on the barbell and lifted the huge weights until they were firmly tucked under his chin, resting on his chest. By this time, he was awash with sweat and the veins on his forehead looked as though they were about to explode. Every single muscle in his body was tightened to the point that they looked as though they were going to snap in two. Would he break the world record? Would he win or would he fail? In a split second he took that bar and thrust it over the top of his head as he screamed at the top of his voice. The crowd erupted as they stood to their feet to give the champion a standing ovation.

With a look of sheer delight, he stepped back as he let the weights crash to the ground. The job was done and the task was complete. He blew a kiss to his proud mother who was looking on from the side of the podium and then lifted his arms in victory as the crowd's applause thundered throughout the arena.

Children, the athlete's greatest strength was not, as the crowd thought, in his ability to lift such heavy weights. His strength was in finding what he was good at. He then spent the time to develop that talent to the point where he achieved good success. Notice that he had to try many things and experience failure many times before finding his true strength. So never be afraid to try something new and never fear failure. A willing student will always benefit from a setback. From it, you can learn some great lessons, which will help you to discover your own strengths. When you discover them, stick with them and then make them even stronger.

More strength to you — Love Dad

THE 10TH LETTER

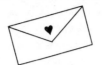

ThE bUcK sToPs WiTh YoU

Responsibility! Tough word. Accountability! Even tougher. Taking charge of your life! *'Now hang on, in just one line of writing you have made me feel very uncomfortable. I'm only a child.'* That may be what you are thinking right now, as you read this letter.

♥

From the age of twelve, I mowed lawns on a weekly basis at the church that both my family and I attended. They had been having trouble maintaining the lawn-mowing roster and so my dad piped up in a church business meeting and volunteered me for the position, saying that he would provide the mower, the tools and the petrol. As a young boy, I was excited, especially knowing that I was going to be the recipient of a weekly payment from the church for my services.

It was tough work for a twelve-year-old and especially in the summer months. The days were hot and the grass was long, but the reward at the end of the day, when I put my invoice in to the church treasurer, was well worth the effort. I soon learnt that even when I didn't feel like mowing the large expanse of lawn, I had a responsibility to do it and to do it well. If I didn't do my part on a Friday afternoon or a Saturday morning, then the people who attended church on Sunday would have to wade through the long grass and be faced with a dishevelled and unkempt scene. I was certain that they would all be in a much happier and a more spiritual state if they arrived to see that the yards were neat and tidy.

Now that I was earning my own income, it was exciting to watch my bank balance grow with every deposit that I made, and at one point I decided that it was the right time to become the proud owner of a bike. When I talked to my parents, I was shocked that they weren't going to buy me one. Now that I was an income producer, it was my responsibility to buy my own. I initially felt that this was completely unfair. All my other friends had received bikes as gifts, even while they were at primary school, while I was still riding my scooter. I suddenly realized that the mountain of money steadily growing in my own personal bank account was going to have to drop in height.

However, once I realized that I was expected to grow up and was settled on that, I caught a bus and visited my local bike shop. I decided I was going to buy a second hand bike, spray paint the frame, remove the rusty accessories and then replace them with brand new ones. I bought transfers to go on the main frame, handle bars that made me look like I was riding a Harley and a light with a generator that ran off the power produced by the bike wheels as they turned. I put on a bike rack and a set of new pedals and once I had finished all the additions, it looked like a brand new bike. I had achieved the result with a lot of effort but for half the price of a new one. This bike would carry me through until I could drive a car. At the same time, I was filled with a sense of pride.

♥

The same feeling of personal responsibility has been repeated time and time again throughout my life. Whenever I have failed in an attempt or have been rejected for my efforts, these have been the times when I have had to reach deep down inside and say, *'It's up to me to turn this thing around. It's no use blaming anyone for my predicament. Life doesn't always dish out what I expect or desire, but right now I have the ability and the power to turn this situation around.'*

You can't stop, in most cases, what circumstances will head your way but you can sure take control of your attitude. Your attitude will make all the difference. It will either make you or break you. Whatever you take on board as you cruise across life's waters will determine whether you sink or swim. So it's up to you to choose.

There are two types of people. Those who are bored and those who have soared. Those who soar get a far better view of what's going on below. It's so much better to have the eye of an eagle than the heart of a chicken. The eagle will rise far above the storms to get a far better perspective of what is really happening below.

When bushwalking, in the depths of a rainforest, I can often only see the canopy, the understory above and the forest floor beneath. Huge vines and creepers weave and wrap their way around the trees that are acting as their hosts. As I climb over the buttress roots of some of the gigantic trees that grace the floor of the forest I will slip on the moss and scrape against the ferns that make this place their home. Unperturbed by the leeches, the different sounds of forest animals and lyre birds as they scratch in the dirt, and the undergrowth, I will trudge on towards my destination. At times my eyes search upwards as I am distracted by the sound of birdlife in the treetops. They are found in the great emergent layer; trees that have thrust their way high above the rest of the forest trees in search of the sunlight. Amidst all this I have complete faith in the little object that I hold securely in my hand; a compass.

It was while I was still a child that I first learnt the skill of orienteering. It was a marvellous experience to be able to track my way home through uncharted territory. It was comforting to know that if I simply obeyed the directives of the compass I would be assured of finding my way without a hitch.

That is how a goal will guide you. Write it down, put a plan in place, which will cause you to apply action to that goal, and then begin. When is the best time to start? Immediately. Do something today that will build towards your goals fulfilment, no matter how small the action may be. The problem with most people is that they only ever think about their goal.

Even those who write their goal down often fail to apply immediate action to it. Immediate action breeds the confidence that one needs to go on to the next step. As Horace wrote, *'He has half the deed done who has made a beginning.'*

I have found this with writing books. By putting down the first word or the first sentence, it wasn't long before I arrived at the first paragraph, then the first page, and then the first chapter. Every single word typed is the key to the book. In the midst of a goal, one needs to divide it up into sizeable bitesize bits. With a book, the first thing I do is to map out a skeletal structure of the book in writing. It's like a map that will be used as my guide for the whole journey of the book until the last page is written.

When you're stuck in the clouds of circumstances, it can be difficult to make clear decisions. That's why we all need goals. They are the compass that will guide you through the valleys, over mountaintops, across rivers, through storm, fire or flood and with that compass in hand you will arrive at your destination safe and sound.

Once the goal is set, this is where the term, *'the buck stops with you'* kicks in. We are responsible for the establishment of our own goals, for the arrival at our own destination, and for the pursuit of our own dreams. It is nobody else's responsibility and we can't go and blame our parents, our friends, our enemies or anyone else for stopping us from pursuing what we have been born to achieve. Even as a child, we are responsible to chart our path. It is never too early to begin and you are never too old to start. Those who determine that the buck stops with them are the ones who will take hold of their future. Guided by the compass of their goals they will eventually arrive at their planned destination. Those who plan are the ones who will ultimately dance all the way to victory.

Let the compass of love guide you
Love Dad

THE 11TH LETTER

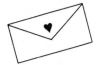

BiG pIe ThInKiNg

Pies. I love them. Apple pies, meat pies, rhubarb pies, lemon meringue pies, mulberry pies, cherry pies and the list goes on and on and on. Your grandma even cooked me a tamarillo and apple pie once. Now that's different. Your great grandma's rhubarb pie though was the best. To put the finishing touch to any sweet pie you have to add a daub of cream or a scoop of delicious ice cream on top to make it just right. On a winter's day, those same pies should always be covered with yellow custard that drips and spills over the edge of the plate. There's also nothing like a good old meat pie and sauce. I love it when the steam ushers the fresh smell of baked pie up and into my nostrils. Sometimes it's hard to determine whether the smell or the taste is best. It's like what happens every time I walk into a coffee shop and smell the aroma of the coffee beans. Sometimes I think I could just get by sniffing coffee rather than drinking it.

I still love reaching into the refrigerator to grab a piece of cold left over apple pie. The pastry has by this time become somewhat soggy but it seems as though the lapsed time between cooking and the eating has made it even more delicious. While my head is stuck inside the fridge, I often search around for the bowl with the leftover cream in it. Quite often, your little fingers have already paved a white trail before me.

I almost forgot. Some of the best pies that we ever made were the mud pies. After a nights rain there was always a lovely puddle left under the swings in the local park, near where I lived. All the kids would love to gather around this puddle and start to mass-produce these mud pies. As a youngster we would imagine that we were having tea and pie for dinner but as we grew older those pies didn't even get a chance to dry before we'd start throwing them at each other.

Then there were the pie graphs that we studied in mathematics, science, commerce and even in geography at school. They would be presented with a range of bright iridescent colours to delineate between the different items that were represented on the chart. More recently, with the use of various computer software, it is always very impressive to see data presented in the form of pie charts by the presenter as he or she clicks a button. New and powerful images are interchanged, added and subtracted onto the screen as they continue to expand the subject they are discussing.

The only challenge I have with the pie chart is that it is always being divided into a finite and fixed amount. My question has always been: What happens when the pie is cut up into as many pieces that can be possibly cut up? I remember how disappointing it was to open the refrigerator door to find that another member of the family had already snatched the last piece of apple pie. The only trace left of the delicious, mouthwatering morsel was a few crumbs or a slithered and shrivelled slice of apple that had somehow escaped the clutches of the hungry intruder.

♥

I believe in big pie thinking. If your pie is your opportunity, your career or your business and you have found it restrictive, then my word to you is this … expand the size of your pie. You are only ever limited or freed by what you think. You have probably heard the term to think outside the circle or to think laterally. These are well and good but I want you to think even bigger and broader than that. Don't allow restrictive thought to bind you up in chains. Seek to build a bigger picture. Begin to see beyond the accepted and refuse to accept the mediocre views of those who speak gloom and doom into every situation.

If your pie is too small or you are running out of pie, look for a bigger one. How do you do this? Well, for one thing I simply start to ask myself a few questions. From a business perspective I ask, How can I do what everybody else is doing, but do it better? How can I better discover what my customers want for their money? What are the trends that are happening in my society today? How can I best use technology to my advantage in business? How can I get others excited about what I have to offer? How can I add value to what I am offering to my clients? How can I create a team atmosphere in my workplace? How can I find a way to encourage those with whom I associate? Is there a way that I can work smarter but still increase my results?

The power is in the questioning. Right now, if you feel that you are stuck in the middle of a small pie, why don't you take some time out and start to write down some questions. The simple art of focussed questioning has the effect of developing a springboard for the answers you require in order to expand your pie.

Develop the attitude that nothing is impossible. There are no restrictions to what you can achieve when the power of belief is released in your life. You not only can produce other pies but you can in fact create bigger pies. So, no matter what you do children, always know that you are in the big pie business.

When someone says you can't, you will reply, *'I can'*. When someone says that you won't, you will respond with a loud, *'I will'*. When others shout it is impossible, you will respond with, *'It is possible'*. When the crowd says it can never be done, you will say, *'It will be done'*. When everyone is out there trying to sell, you will be there to buy. When the air is filled with the word shortage, you will be discussing the oversupply. When there is lack, you will speak of abundance. When there is war, you will be heralding peace. You will be the fish who swims upstream. You will be the wall that stems the tide. You will be the lighthouse, firmly planted on the solid rock, telling the huge liners to move out of your way.

For you will be in the big pie business. These pies will never run out because the power of creation is within you and the power of questioning is being developed and enhanced through practice day by day. You respect the facts but are guided by your heart and your intuition. You are guided not by sight but by the spirit of faith. For every gloom and doom, you see the sunshine. For every tragedy, you see the recovery. For every failure, you see the success. Some will say that you see the world through rosy tinted glasses but in fact, you see the storms of life through the eye of the rainbow. The spectre is replaced by the spectrum. Every death provides room for a new life.

When people ask you what business you are in, you will herald, *'I am in the Big Pie Business. I love pies. I make pies. I eat pies. I enjoy pies and when the crumbs are left on the pie plate I simply roll up my sleeves and make another pie. My pies are ever expanding pies. There is no limit to the size of the pies that come out of my life and my mind because I think big, I eat big, I give big and I live big. I expect to find big pies wherever I go and I refuse to be restricted by the small pie thinkers who live around me. I am spreading the message of the big pie to everyone I meet, because we live in the most exciting time in history. It is the time of the big pie'.*

♥

Mmmm! Children, I'm sorry to report that if you go to the fridge tomorrow to find the rest of that nice apple pie mum cooked for us tonight, well I just couldn't resist it. There are a few crumbs left but being big pie thinkers I know it won't take you long to get another one in there.

Love you in a big way
Dad

THE 12TH LETTER

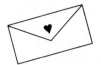

PaY aTtEnTiOn To DeTaIl

Children, at times I have watched you as you have spent hours filling out every minute detail on a picture you are drawing for me. I have also observed you inviting bears to share in the lunch that you have prepared for them with your imaginary food and drink. You take great care with the way you position your teddy bears on your bed before you set off for school. Your concentration is amazing as you design a letter for me and then take the time to fold it in an origami fashion, so that the letter is a very special gift. The birthday cards, whether prepared freehand or designed on our computer, always give me a sense of joy because of the care and the love taken by you to prepare such a beautiful gift.

As I chip away at writing this letter to you, I am like a sculptor forming a beautiful statue out of a solid piece of marble. However, the marble in my case is made from thousands of words, which I carefully choose as I put them down, one by one, onto the page. As a writer, my first job is to put words to paper. As I write I am not concerned with grammar or spelling (thank goodness I have spell check on my computer. My first attempts at writing were rather painstaking as I punched my first manuscripts on an old typewriter). My prime concern, when I write, is to get a volume of thoughts onto the page. In fact, I aim at putting at least 1,000 words down every day. I generally start writing early in the morning, before I am distracted by tele-phone calls; and on most days, I hit the goal but there are times when my writing is flowing so well that I outstrip it. By setting a daily goal I have forced myself to stretch for it. By having the goal in place I have a better chance of hitting than I have of missing. My ultimate goal is to complete another book of letters that will bless you, along with many other people.

The true art of sculpturing words begins once I have all the words down on paper. I have to take hold of the manuscript and word by word, paragraph by paragraph, mould and shape it through the editorial process. This is where an average piece of writing can be transformed into a masterpiece. I have other editors working on it as well and with a combination of input I can begin to pay attention to the minute detail that will make my book an easy read. As someone once said about good books, *'An easy read is the result of a hard write.'*

It's all about paying close attention to details. It is a vital quality for success. How wonderful you feel when you know that you have completed a task to the best of your ability. You are proud of the sweat that you have poured out in the pursuit of your goal. The energy expended, through thinking or phys-ical effort, to produce a result, fills you with a sense of great satisfaction. I have found that no matter what I do, whether it is for a client, for my family or for a friend, that if I have made it my goal to pay attention to detail I will always be filled with a sense of pride and achievement.

We must develop the ability to look beneath the surface and to look further than others. To dot every 'i' and to cross every 't' is what it is all about. To leave no stone unturned is important because everything that you do has a value higher than the job itself.

♥

This reminds me of the old story of the three little pigs, because in the administration of detail we are in fact constructing something that is built to last.

All the little pigs must have known that there would come

a time when they would be surely tested by the wily wolf. Yet, for some reason one of the pigs decided to construct his house with straw. Why did he choose straw? Could it have been for price or ease of construction?

The second little pig built his house with sticks. If he happened to have lived near a wooded area, these sticks would have been easy to obtain. If it was a cold night, I suppose that the pig wouldn't need to venture from the house. He could in fact pluck a stick or two out of the walls and use them for the fire. The walls could be easily replaced at any time. It too would have required a lot less time to build.

However the third pig, in designing a brick house, would have required the assistance of an architect and the aid of professional builders. The bricks would have been bought at a much higher price than the materials used by the other two pigs. Then there was the mortar and the cement to put in a secure foundation. The whole process would have taken a much longer period to construct than the other two shanties. In fact, the third pig may have been extremely disadvantaged for a time, even having to live with the relatives while waiting for the construction process to be totally completed.

The need for closer attention to detail would have required some painstaking work. When the other two pigs were well and truly finished, they probably watched on as the third pig waited on the completion of his solid home.

Attention to detail always requires concentrated effort. Add to this a dose of extra determination to see the task through until its completion.

Then the wolf came. They had heard of the wolf and had in fact seen the wolf from a distance. However, most of the piggy community said that his howl was worse than his height, or was that his bark was worse than his bite (no that was the local farmer's dog.) Because of that, they were a little lack-adaisical in their attitude towards the beady-eyed creature whose brother had already gobbled up Red Riding Hood's grandmother in another fairytale.

Knowing that the straw house was going to be a piece of cake to remove, he huffed and he puffed and in fact sent straw flying all over the neighbouring field. The cows were greatly appreciative as they watched the little pig inhabitant run all the way to the second pig's house, made of sticks.

Well you probably know the rest of the story. Not being totally satisfied with the results obtained at the straw address, the wolf quickly moved over to the wooden house, or more correctly termed the stick house.

He huffed and he puffed and before he had a chance to take a final breath the two little pigs ran out the front door. They escaped just in time to look back to see the stick house burst into flames. The sticks had tumbled onto the stove where the little pig had just put a kettle on to make a fresh cup of tea for the highly stressed pig number one.

Where to from there? Straight to the house that was built to detailed plans and specifications: the house that had taken much longer to build than the other two houses.

The funny thing is that although you may have heard otherwise, the wolf didn't even bother about this one because his brother in law had drawn up the plans. He knew that the structure of such a building would easily withstand the breath of any wolf and there was no way he was going to climb down any old chimney. So, he turned and took off again into the wood and decided to have a salad sandwich for lunch - minus the ham.

Pay attention to detail and you won't fail
Love Dad

THE 13TH LETTER

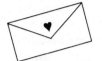

Be ThRiFtY

In this day and age of home based businesses there are so many available opportunities to build successful businesses without all the trappings of big business. Now I know that this doesn't relate to many of the retail businesses that fill the marketplace and if you want to go into retail, that's fine. However, it is an established fact that as we continue to forge new ground in the IT industry, there will be an ever-increasing number of cottage based industries rising from the third or fourth bedroom of many homes throughout the world.

I recall starting my first 'real' business in my bedroom as an eighteen-year-old. I was working for a wholesale jeweller at the time and had decided to buy my own stock with my earnings. I started making up jewellery pieces that I could sell to neighbours and friends. It was a great time to start business because it was just before Christmas. I remember the night that my father's sister-in-law brought a few friends with her and they spent quite a lot on the trinkets that I had prepared.

In my twenties, I started a business with a partner. Our first office was run out of the garage attached to the house we were living in at the time. We then had grandiose ideas of expanding into an area of prime commercial real estate with great exposure along with all the trappings. It wasn't too long, after we had successfully spent a lot of money on carpets, office walls, partitions, curtains, alarm systems and the like, that we suddenly realized that with the products and services we were providing, we had probably bitten off more than we could chew. From that day on until the lease expired we were constantly digging ourselves out of a financial hole. We had overextended, overexpanded, overborrowed and overrun what was commonsense and practicable.

Now, I am not against nice offices and well presented premises but if you can run your business, without all the trappings, choose it. There are many other ways that you can impress a client rather than by having a plush office. Here's a few: professional service, professional presentation in the way you dress, a professional telephone manner (see the 4th letter), and by being someone who delivers what they promise. These four alone can in most cases get the job done just as effectively. Learn to live within your means. Focus on developing a greater income than you have expenditure. Now I know that in setting up a new business there are times when you will have to stretch, but only stretch as far as you can quickly recover in the shortest possible time. Don't overextend beyond reason and whatever you do, if you're going to spend money, ask yourself this question. Is what I'm doing right now going to get a return on my expenditure in a reasonable timeframe or is this just one of those trappings that will ultimately lead to excessive debt?

I've learnt one thing in business and that is, if you are simply out to impress then all you may end up with is a bill. Having the trappings of success and a maxed credit card will only carry you for so long. What you need to have is the mind of a cutter and the attitude of a trimmer. Always ask yourself, how can I do this better and achieve even better results at less cost?

It is probably best summarized in the word thriftiness. To be thrifty is the moral obligation of every man and woman. This is not only in the area of finances but also in the area of time. If you use your time and finances wisely there will be no need for you to ever lack the good things that life has to offer you.

Integrity is probably number one on my list if you are going to experience long term success but close following that is thriftiness; always keeping your expenditure within your income.

J.C. Penney once said, *'In training men we always start them on a small salary, partly because we want to see how they will manage on it. If he finds ways and means to eliminate waste in his own affairs, to practice economy, to get good value for every dollar of his income, it is fairly safe to conclude that he will be able to run a business on those same sound principles.'* He went on to say that, *'some managers, for example, want to buy a home or an automobile with the profits of the first year or two of the business. They do not realize that, though they have earned their dividend, the profits must stay in the business until it has flourished sufficiently to warrant the drawing out of a few thousand dollars.'*

Your goal in running your business should be to have fewer people managing more assets because profits are a much better indicator of a businesses health than size.

The backbone of any successful business is your ability to provide good service. If you can do that, you won't ever look back.

As you seek to grow a business from it's inception, never despise small beginnings, nor small profits, for they are the very foundation of big success. Never spend all what you earn. If you can keep your expenditure lower than your earnings, you are on the road to becoming rich. It is far more profitable to pay wages than to ever receive them. Always look for opportunities to delegate. No use spending time on something that someone else is capable of doing. Remember your time is money and if something doesn't necessarily need to be done now, then don't do it.

Look to buy and look for new and uncharted territory but if you need to venture where others have already been, do it better than the rest. Make it your goal to excel, to outstrip and to outrun. Outserve and outgive your competition.

Whatever you do, don't blow your own trumpet. Someone else is always looking for ways to adopt the tune that you're playing. Keep your successes to yourself. Not only is it prudent but it is also wisdom.

Make love the backbone of all you do. Always forgive.

Don't listen to the accolades that men will give you once you start to experience success. Listen to your own voice within and if you know that you have done well, let that be enough to carry you on to the next success.

Make "mistakes" your teacher, not your enemy, and be a diligent student of the ones you have made and of the ones others have made.

Learn the skills of handling money. Turn your savings into capital and seek out ways to cause that capital to grow. It is an art and it is a skill worthy to be learnt. Unfortunately, it is known by only a small percentage who live upon this earth. Make it your ambition to rule money rather than having it rule you. It is a tool that can be used for great good. So use it wisely, use it well.

As your wealth and skill increase, your expenses will grow much slower until eventually they will cease growing, thus allowing you to increase your capital.

Make your most strenuous labour the labour of thinking. I personally seek many ways to get out of having to remain in my office. It is by the sea, in the mountains, or in a park, with book in hand and pen and notepad at the ready, that I receive my greatest inspiration. I take my office with me wherever I go in order to find those thoughts that will carry me to the next strongest position in business.

Wealth is available for you and is a mighty tool with which you can do much good. Learn the value of it as a child. Don't spend all you earn. Give ten per cent. Save ten per cent and invest as much as you can. Make it your goal to study, to learn, to experiment and to pursue ways to richly bless the world. Lift people in all your endeavours and then the acquisition of money will take care of itself.

Never short on love
Love Dad

THE 14TH LETTER

RiSk It

The difference between the hare and the tortoise is this: the tortoise took the greatest risk. He stuck his neck out so much further. In the natural scene of events, and with the tortoise's track history, the hare was going to outstrip, outwhip, outrun and convincingly beat the tortoise. In the time that the tortoise could have completed the course, the hare could have done it a dozen times, running backwards and with his eyes blindfolded. A little far-fetched you might say, but from a design point of view, it was like matching up a Ferrari, red in colour (because they always go faster) with a child's dinky. They were mismatched and the result was a foregone conclusion. The bookies would have had the odds for the tortoise at a 1,000 to 1 because the hare, in their eyes, was a sure thing.

It was tough coming from a lineage of losers; well that was the story the hares passed around in their exclusive circles. It was well known that hares were winners and tortoises were losers. It had been like that for generations and as far as they were concerned, it was going to stay that way from now to eternity. God made hares fast and God made tortoises slow. That was it, adfinitum.

Only the older generation of tortoises could remember the first time a tortoise ever challenged a hare to a race. The hare beat that small tortoise by a mile. Many were embarrassed. However, some remembered how that tortoise crossed the finish line. The crowds had all gone home and the sun was slowly setting in the western sky. His feet were swollen and cut, he was dehydrated and there were only a few faithful friends and family waiting. They had waited throughout the long hot day to finally cheer him across the finish line. They were proud. He had finished the race.

Even as the tortoise had struggled to make the distance, he was planning his next assault on haredom. He knew that if you wanted to win then you had to step out of the maddening crowd, hang on to hope, draw on the dream and put everything you've got into what you believe. If he was unable to beat the hare himself then he would find one, younger than he, with the spirit of a leopard. He would search for the one who would dare to face the taunts of the masses who kept telling him that it could never be done. He had decided to become the coach of the next generation.

♥

Year after year, as he came across younger tortoises with a twinkle in their eye, he would invite them to join a growing group of tortoises who planned and strategized to find a way to once and for all break their losing pattern. His dream was to have recorded in the history books, for all future young tortoises, of a time when a tortoise beat a hare. They needed to know that there was a time when a tortoise stuck his neck out, threw down the gauntlet and decided to smash through the barrier that had held tortoisedom in the grips of low self esteem for thousands of years. It was time to crash, as it were, through the sound barrier, through the speed of light barrier, through the four-minute mile barrier, through all those things that had limited their thinking for so long.

They were an unlikely bunch of tortoises. Being young, many of them at first were unkempt in appearance. The older tortoise though was the one who gave the group of young dreamers the impetus and the inspiration to even dare to reach beyond what any tortoise had ever reached. It wasn't long before the discipline of training started to transform these carefully selected tortoises into a team of athletes. They knew that only one tortoise could be chosen for the big event but they all recognized that each had a part to play in the success of this venture. If one won they would all win.

On a Saturday night, after each week of training, they would gather at the elder tortoise's house. He would tell them great stories about animals that were even faster than the hare. He talked of the lioness and the gazelle. He talked of running with grace and with speed and their favourite chant was, *'Run like the wind, run like the wind, we can run like the wind.'* At the end of each session every week, they began to notice how they were starting to move just that little bit faster. Even the tortoises that had a reputation for slow learning were starting to excel in their subjects at school.

Every afternoon they would practice, practice, practice moving just a little swifter, thinking a little quicker and smarter. They were convinced that one of their group would not only finish but would in fact win. They weren't thinking like tortoises. They were all eagles. They saw themselves running faster than before. They were the leaves that were plucked from branches in the storm, buffeted into the air and blown away in a matter of seconds to a neighbouring field. They were the tornado and the blizzard. They were the ones who were going to change the thinking of every tortoise and hare that lived on the face of the earth for the rest of all time. They were history makers and world shakers. They never talked about being slow because they were always talking about being on the go, by staying in the flow.

It was not unusual to catch one of the group racing a butterfly or chasing a grasshopper. Throughout all their training the old coach kept detailed records of their progress, never promising who would be the one to challenge the hare, but simply encouraging a healthy team spirit with the philosophy, if one wins we all win.

The coach though had come under some vicious verbal attacks from his generation of tortoises. They said, *'How can you expect to win? You never did. What right have you to think that you can find a tortoise that is faster than a hare? What if they fail? You could ruin the life of a young tortoise forever. He'll be scarred for life.'* One old tortoise even accused him of setting up a sect that would twist the young minds of these tortoises who attended his sessions. Another claimed that he was inciting a revolution amongst tortoises. Their attacks were relentless. But ignoring them, the coach kept to his plan and formed a team with a winning attitude.

The day finally arrived and all tortoisedom and haredom gathered for the heralded event that had captured the hearts and minds of the animal kingdom. It seemed that everyone had turned up because the word on the street was that the tortoises had developed some secret weapon. The hares simply laughed it off because they knew that no matter what a tortoise could do, they could never beat a hare.

When the officials checked on the history of hare and tortoise racing, they found that one of the competitors had the right of choosing the course to be run. A hare had chosen the last course. A tortoise would choose it this time. The coach knew of this and declared that it was to be a downhill race, a sprint to the finish line.

The coach, to everyone's surprise, chose the slowest of the tortoises from the group of athletes. Unperturbed, they realized that the coach knew exactly what he was doing and settled down to cheer on their fellow athlete.

A hush came across the animals as the official starter stepped up into the starting box. The hare crouched, prepared to win yet another race, while the little slow tortoise moved himself into a side on position at the line. Everybody gasped saying, *'What do you think he's doing? He's heading in the wrong direction. What a stupid tortoise, he doesn't even know where the finish line is?'*

The gun went off and the hare shot quickly out of the starting blocks. As the crowd looked on, the tortoise's head and legs suddenly disappeared. The shell began to rock quickly from side to side. Suddenly it started to tumble down the hill, getting closer and closer to the speeding hare, ever gaining in velocity. The shell bounced higher and higher with every bounce. The crowds shouting ceased as they witnessed the amazing spectacle. The hare took one quick glance behind him to see a tortoise shell heading straight for his head. He ducked.

By the time he had turned his head towards the finishing line, the tortoise shell burst through the winners tape. It then landed on a pile of soft cabbage leaves that had been strategically positioned by the rest of the coach's team.

♥

Well children, you may never have heard this story before, but you may have heard the one where a tortoise beat another hare. He was so inspired by this story that he thought he could win as well. Do you know what, the hare fell asleep and the tortoise won? Different strategy, same result!

Never be afraid of taking a risk
Love Dad

See the storms
of life
through the eye
of the
rainbow.

THE 15TH LETTER

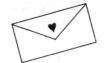

ChEcK yOuR sOuRcE

Have you ever watched a droplet of water at night? From our living room, when the rain begins to fall, we are able to see drops of water hitting the top of a wall that borders an adjacent courtyard. When they hit, and if you see it from the right angle, each single droplet catches a beam of light in its path. With every drop, there is a little light explosion. It is a mini light show; nature's dance display performed just for us by each descending droplet.

Millions of these water droplets congregate, from within the great catchment areas that surround the rivers of our world, to form rushing torrents. The source of any great river should determine the quality of the water as it reaches its journeys end. However, as has been documented time and time again, with the increased population that spreads its net along the banks of many of these great rivers, we find that water is not the only thing being added to the rush and the flow. Contaminates such as effluent from sewerage and litter from the streets find their way into the waterways to change what was once pure and clean into something harmful to human life.

The rivers that grace our planet provide homes for multitudinous numbers of fish, water birds and other river creatures. They provide water for animals and for humanity, whether for drinking or for the irrigation of crops. To do that in a profitable and beneficial manner, it is always important to be assured that the source is providing nothing but the freshest supply of water.

Webster's dictionary explains source as: the place from which anything comes or is obtained. This reminds me of the phrase, *'Garbage in, garbage out'*, a term coined many years ago with particular reference to the computer. This can also be applied to our bodies. For in this past century the stature and physique of humankind has changed. We're getting taller and we're living longer because of the radical changes that have occurred in dietary intake and in the world of medicine.

The same principle applies to our minds. The source of information that we tap into will greatly influence the way we think and the way we act. It is so important to guard what we allow into our minds because it can be the source of our prosperity and happiness or the source of misery. It's our choice.

I recently visited a local dam, which is not more than fifteen minutes from where I now live. I particularly like going there after it has just rained because I can be assured of seeing a good steady flow of water over the edge of the dam. There is something fascinating about watching the water as it falls down, down, down on its continued journey to the smaller stream below. At the top of the dam there always seems to be at least one log that resists the temptation of taking the downward plunge. I watch it closely, wishing that a gust of wind would splash a wave up against it. I'd love to see it join the rest of the debris found at the bottom of the dam.

There is yet another dam, which is a little further away from where I live. On this particular day, I decided to stop off at the bottom, where the water would generally flow into the valley. It is a very impressive structure. The dam wall, unlike most of the other dams I have seen before, has a huge wall constructed of large rocks and pieces of gravel. This adjoins the normal cement structure. It is through here that the excess water is released from time to time. After making my way down a set of stairs, I entered a concrete corridor that actually took me under the spillway. At equal intervals along the enclosed corridor there were window openings from which I could see the water below.

The closer I walked to the end of the corridor I noticed an increasingly stronger smell of fish. People were fishing below but it wasn't the smell of the fish they'd caught that was filling the air. There were dozens and dozens of fish floating on the surface of the water and they were piled on each side of the reedy and rocky lagoon. The stench increased the closer I came towards the devastating scene.

I found it hard to believe that people would still be fishing in such an environment. They were adamant that these fish had died because of lack of oxygen in the still waters, but I wondered if there was another reason. It looked a long way from the top of the dam to the bottom. I don't know about the fish, but if I'd been bashed by rushing water against the cement walls of the dam, I'd be just as stunned. The other question was, could it be possible that the waters had some form of contaminates in them?

♥

Stringent control measures are necessary to ensure that the source of our drinking water arrives uncontaminated. In recent times, even these have failed in many metropolitan centres. Many families have realized that they can't always rely on the source and have then taken responsibility for their own health by installing water filters in their households.

In our day to day lives, we need to take the same care in filtering out any negatives that might seek to infiltrate our lives. We need to ensure that we source positive and uplifting, champion building and mind expanding information that will lead us towards the fulfilment of our dreams.

♥

When I lived in Sydney as a child, my family would regularly visit Warragamba Dam. It was a great place for a picnic and we loved it. There was always hot water on tap for mum and dad's cups of tea and plenty of barbecue facilities. The lawns were well manicured and there were park areas to run around in, and plenty of beautiful trees to shade us from the hot sun. We would always climb on the play equipment and grab the chance to look at the dam in full working order.

After a satisfying barbecue, we would usually play a game of cricket. I loved to hit the ball into a fountain that was located in the middle of one of the parks. It would be fun to watch dad trying to fish it out. The water, as it spurted upwards from the middle of the fountain, would generally push the ball to the side for those who were patient. For those less patient, a water fight would culminate with one or all of us being doused with a splash of cool water. On hot days, we didn't mind it at all. The more times the ball landed in the fountain the better.

After that, we would pack up all our picnic gear and head off on a walk down to the dam. Just walking across the dam was an experience in itself: to see the vast layers of concrete below and as they stretched up each side of the dam; to see the mighty expanse of water that was held back by the dams walls; to see, if we had timed our visit right, the dams gates being opened.

It was a mar ellous sight to see thousands upon thousands of litres of water released into the valley below. When that was happening, the best view was from the suspension bridge that was strung further down the valley. A wooden structure, it was quite scary as it swayed with every step taken. You could even see the valley floor below through the wide spaces between the wooden planks. Once you stopped looking beneath and you focussed on the dam and the spurting water, it made the whole adventure extremely worthwhile.

Not only did the source of this great dammed river supply fresh water to the metropolitan area but like many dams, it also supplied electricity to many homes.

Children, safeguard your lives by making positive friendships with dreamers and achievers. Drink from only the clear pristine waters of inspirational books, tapes and seminars. Drink from those whom you can proudly call mentors. You will then speak to others and they in turn will be refreshed by one who has checked their source. You!

Thank you for being my source of joy
Love Dad

A successful life
first sees
and then does.

THE 16TH LETTER

YoU cAn

'*I think I can, I think I can.*' These famous words are now etched in the minds of countless thousands around the world. '*I think I can, I think I can*' rings in my ears whenever I have the opportunity of riding in a train. As I close my eyes all I can hear, over and over again, are those words, '*I think I can, I think I can.*' Each word keeps in time with the sound of the wheels as they race along the railway tracks. '*I think I can, I think I can.*'

♥

Drift back with me, if you will, to a lonely countryside, where the sun was shining, and the fresh breath of spring was blowing across the face of the earth. The flowers were blooming, the newly born lambs gambolled in the fields while bumping occasionally into their mothers for a fresh drink of milk or for security and assurance. The grass was fresh and green from the light rains that had fallen the night before and the air was filled with the sounds of insects and birdsong. The scene was bursting with new life and vibrancy.

Suddenly, the air was shattered by the sound '*Choo, choo, choo, choo, choo, choo, choo, choo,*' with an intermittent burst from a train whistle that caused all the animals to turn their heads. As the source of the noise appeared, all that could be heard across the fields, apart from the whistle, were the sounds of the animals saying under their breath, '*Oh, it's only that silly little engine again.'*

The little engine unfortunately had quite a reputation for disturbing the peace and was renowned for showing off from time to time. He was always trying to impress somebody, somewhere. He was not at all popular amongst the bigger engines and in fact, because of his unpredictable behaviour, his circle of friends had depleted somewhat during the past year.

What the big engines didn't like about him was that he would always play tricks on them. Like the time he stopped at the southern end of a dark tunnel, unbeknown to the larger engine that was travelling in the opposite direction. As soon as it reached the northerly end of the tunnel the little engine turned on its lights and tooted, *'Surprise!'*, causing the large engine to pull back hard on his brakes. He pulled so hard that he buckled the rails while screeching and sliding through the tunnel, finally stopping within a metre of the little engine.

Then there was the other time. During the night, while all the big engines were fast asleep, he rearranged the whole yard by moving empty carriages into position, so that in the morning all the big engines were blocked in and were unable to move. It took them hours to unravel the confusion the little engine had caused. To top it off, while they were trying to sort out the mess, the little engine was sound asleep in an adjacent yard.

His favourite trick was to sneak up quietly behind an old grandfather engine as he dozed off during his lunchtime. He would let off a mighty peep from his whistle and it frightened the old timers so much that they just about jumped up and off their tracks. In fact, there was a time when one was actually derailed.

However, a lot of this misbehaviour arose out of the fact that the little engine really wanted to grow up and become a big engine. He would watch as they pulled heavy loads of coal from the coalmines and how others would pull long loads of containers that had been taken from a ship at the nearby port. Then there were those who travelled interstate, carrying hundreds of passengers. Even the daily city trains would go back and forth all day taking both young and old humans to their destinations. He just wanted to be noticed and to be appreciated for who he was.

When he offered to do some of the tasks that the big engines were accustomed to doing, he would constantly hear, *'You can't do that, you're only a little engine,'* or *'Only big engines do that sort of job. Clear off!'*

Day after day, he would simply run errands, transport small packages or shuttle empty carriages from one large engine to another. Life was always busy but he never found it to be too demanding. A nagging thought also kept flashing across his mind, *'I wonder if I'll ever get the chance to do something significant or something really important?'*

However, as day passed into another day and as one year pushed aside another year, the opportunity never seemed to present itself. The bigger and more handsome engines quickly snapped up whatever important job would come along. Little engines were never considered.

This constant state of rejection started to take it's toll on both the inside and the outside of the little engine and it wasn't long before his shiny and sprightly appearance was starting to show neglect. Paint was peeling off the side of his funnel and spots of rust were starting to form on sections of his main body. He'd lost his spark and the tricks he used to play were lost to memory. He was rarely called upon to do any duties, and in fact he had been shuttled into the back section of the yard. He was left to rust and gather dust.

However, there came a day when a new little engine came to visit. This engine was unique because it wasn't a 'he' but was in fact a 'she'. Now apart from the carriages, it was quite a rare sight to find a female engine in this neck of the woods. So there were plenty of whistles and bells ringing as she sauntered up the main track and let off an impressive puff of steam when she arrived. Not only was she pretty but she was in fact a 'motorvational speaker' who had been brought in to revitalize the whole yard. It had lost its spark. Production was down. Performance was slack and the entire place needed a good shake-up.

Word filtered throughout the whole rail yard and even ventured as far as the back blocks where the little engine was moping; regretting the day he had ever been manufactured. However, at that moment a tiny thought came to him: just a spark of inspiration that caused a rattle in his engine and a movement in his wheels. '*What if I could catch the attention of the little female engine?*' As soon as the thought had appeared it had gone again. '*No, she'd be far more impressed by the larger and more prominent engines. They strut up and down the platforms every day. They pull huge loads and flex their enormous muscles. What would a pretty engine ever want with a rusty little dilapidated engine like me?*' However, he thought that at least he could go and see what this new engine looked like. From what he had heard, she sounded pretty special.

A special meeting of all the engines had been arranged that evening in the largest enclosure in the yard, so that just about all the engines could be present. Tickets had sold extremely fast and by the time the little engine had a chance to dust himself down and oil his aching joints, every ticket had been sold. Undeterred by this turn of events he decided he would go anyway.

The air was filled with smoke from the hundreds of engines who had turned up to hear their first 'motorvational' speech ever. Fortunately for the little engine, as he stood on the fringe of the crowd, they had installed a sound system so that he could at least catch a word here and a word there. He couldn't see her but was fortunate enough to have caught a glimpse of one of the promotional flyers that had been passed around with her picture on it. She was gorgeous in an engine sort of way: big eyes and long eyelashes. As she spoke, her voice was filled with emotion and was full of energy. It seemed to even cheer him up.

It was probably only twenty minutes into the speech when an emergency announcement cut across the loud speaker system. '*A runaway carriage is heading towards the township. It has become disconnected and if not stopped it will crash into the village, threatening life.*' Now because all the engines were crammed in to hear the speaker, the only one able to respond immediately was the little engine.

He took off quickly in the direction of the runaway carriage. It was inconceivable that the little engine would have any chance of catching it, let alone stopping it. It was much larger than he was.

However, he was past worrying about that. He had to do something. He was the only one who could get there quick enough. As he came over the hill from the east and raced through the station of the small township that could possibly, in a few moments be the scene of a terrible disaster, he could see the thundering carriage speeding down the hill from the west. He had decided that the best way to stop the carriage was to stop and then gradually speed back towards the station. This would allow the carriage to attach itself on to him and then he could gradually slow down. Hopefully it would lessen the impact.

So that is what he did. However, when the carriage reached the little engine it hit with such force that the little engine was very nearly forced off the track. The smell of his brakes filled the air with a pungent smell as he tried with all his might to slow the carriage. Above the screeching and the smoke rose the screams of the passengers as they considered their fate. Rushing closer and closer to the station the strain was evident as the screws from the little engines body began to pop and as it slid and screeched along the tracks trying desperately to slow down. To everyone's amazement, as the smoke continued to pour not only from the little engines funnel, but also from his wheels, the carriage slowly but surely came to a complete stop.

That was not the end of it. The little engine then began to say, *'I think I can, I think I can, I think I can, I think I can.'* All the passengers and all the staff at the station watched on as this dilapidated and rusty little engine began to push the carriage back to where it had come from. He was going to make sure that the people could continue on their original journey. With every hill they traversed, they could hear, *'I think I can, I think I can, I think I can.'* He didn't stop until he had joined the carriage with the original engine and the carriages that it had become separated from.

A heroes welcome was given to the little engine, and guess who gave him the heroes kiss? You guessed it, the beautiful 'motorvational' speaker. All the big engines looked on with envy.

He was later given a complete overhaul and then invited to chaperone her all over the country on all her speaking engagements. He was once and for all freed from the humdrum existence that was eked out by the larger engines.

Motor on little engines, because you can

Love Dad

THE 17TH LETTER

BeFrIeNd An ExPeRt

Everybody is an expert. Everybody has a talent that has been divinely bestowed upon him or her when they were born.

I remember that as a child, there were children in my class who were experts in maths. Others were experts in spelling. There were expert soccer players and expert dancers, expert actors, expert readers and so on went the list. Everybody, I discovered, was good at something.

What are you good at? What is a major strength in your life? What are you an expert in, or better still, what area of life do you wish to become an expert in?

Anyway, what is an expert? My Webster's dictionary calls an expert: one whom is experienced, taught by use or practice; skillful; dexterous; adroit; having a facility of operation or performance from practice.

Your grandfather was an expert in creating things around the home. He was always doing something new or changing something around the house, whether it was a garden or an addition, an adjustment of a window or a room. There was always something going on. Nothing ever stood still. There was always some project happening and our household was always in a constant state of change.

I suppose that this creative ability, which he wielded with a measure of ease, eventually rubbed off onto his son. Whereas my creativity lies in the use of words and in the area of music, his related to the use of his hands and in the area of manual labour.

He also had the ability of drawing others in to assist him to achieve the jobs that needed to be completed. Although he always worked the longest and the hardest, he was able to command the assistance of others because he was a giver in his own right.

Whenever there was a working bee or a task needing completion at the local church, your grandfather was always there in the thick of things, either painting or putting something together. He was reliable and he was an expert who finished what he set out to do each time.

♥

Our reactions to our Dad's instructions change throughout the years. It is a well-known fact that as a child you think your dad knows everything. By the time you're a teenager, you start to wonder whether he knows anything at all. When you hit your twenties and early thirties, you are now quite convinced that he really doesn't know what he's talking about. But then as the years press on you suddenly realize that maybe your Dad held within his life some gems of wisdom. Maybe it's a good thing to start digging them up and applying them. In fact, if you had started applying them a little earlier you may have saved yourself a few detours throughout the years.

♥

In business today I now seek experts in different fields, whether it be in the financial, intellectual, spiritual, social or physical areas of my life, but when it comes to day to day practical living I keep coming back to the basic principles that your grandfather taught me as a child. I call them life principles. I don't think he ever verbally explained these to me, but by his example I picked them up by osmosis. They may seem simplistic. However, in some ways the simplicity of these guidelines is wherein the power lies. There were probably lots more lessons that he taught me but these are the ones that stand out to me at this time.

♥

a)   **Always finish what you start**

b)   **If you do something do it well**

c)   **Take good care of your health**

d)   **Don't neglect your spiritual life**

e)   **Keep neat and tidy**

f)   **Obey directions**

g)   **Help others**

h)   **Always use the best tools**

♥

a)   **Always finish what you start**

It would be unthinkable to even consider the following scenario. It is the Olympics. Lined up on the starting line are the most elite athletes in the world. They are all in contention to beat the 100-metre world track record. As soon as the starting gun is fired, each of the contestants decides that just for a change they will run in different directions. One is off to the discus area. Another heads off on a marathon and runs out of the stadium. Another dodges the javelins as they are being thrown while another one lies down and goes to sleep. Yet how often do individuals do that very same thing with their lives? They begin with a grandiose goal and start in tremendous fashion but fail to remember that a goal set is a goal to be met. Now, it is true that sometimes you may have set the wrong goal or that you have found yourself unsuited to that particular venture. The important thing though is that when you reset it, don't quit until it's done.

b) **If you do something do it well**

I noticed one thing about your grandfather. Everything he sought to do, he did well. Now, he may have lacked the skills at times but he was never afraid to learn or to try. At the end of the day you could look at what he had done and say that it had been done with a touch of excellence. It looked great. There were times when he had to innovate and adapt but at the end of a job, it was always done well.

c) **Take good care of your health**

Do you know that your grandfather never told me to not drink or smoke? Not once. He just took me to visit my relatives who smoked like chimneys and drank like fish. That was enough to scare any young child. I then observed through the years as some died from emphysema and how some marriages and lives were ripped apart in the midst of lifestyles that included those ingredients.

In fact, it is because of those negative examples that I have such a keen interest in healthy living. I know that it's not only those two things that cause harm to the human body and mind, but it has become more and more evident how important it is to keep a healthy lifestyle. We need to eat correctly, get regular exercise, and take sufficient hours for rest and recreation so that we can have the energy and the corresponding enthusiasm to go about our daily duties.

I can still remember how our relatives used to knock your grandfather and laugh at him because he was the only one drinking soft drinks on Christmas Day. I wonder who has the last laugh today? It's not just about drinking and smoking, it's in fact about maintaining a healthy lifestyle that will give you the best chance to live long and to live well.

d) **Don't neglect your spiritual life**

This is all about developing good habits. Now we all know that going to church doesn't mean you are a Christian, but I do know that by having the habit of being exposed to a positive environment I had a better chance of getting the right input into my life. I was more likely to find that at church than I was down at the local pub. I met my Lord there, I met my wife there and I now take my children there. It's worth checking out a good Bible believing church and get involved.

e) **Keep neat and tidy**

You can tell a lot about a man by the way he takes care of his shoes, of his car and of his yard. I must confess that I learn a lot about someone when I look at his or her shoes. If they take care of their footwear, it means that they pay attention to detail in their lives. The car is the same. Particularly the inside and back seat floor area. How many packets of McDonalds chip cartons are still lying there? The state of someone's yard will reveal the same. They are only little things but a clean environment speaks of a clean and tidy mind. I'm not encouraging that you should go and do a shoe, car and yard inspection of all your friends, but what we generally see on the outside is a clear representation of what's happening on the inside of someone else's life. As a man thinks in his heart so is he. I like to do business with someone who is taking care of his personal affairs because I know that they will more than likely reflect this attribute in their business affairs.

f) **Obey Directions**

Someone who can follow instructions and fulfil directions will soon be in a position where they can start giving them themselves. To be a leader you first need to be a good follower, so obey directions.

g) **Help others**

To be the greatest, first learn to be a servant. The reason people flocked to help your grandfather was because he was always giving of himself freely to others. It's a fine quality and one that we all need to demonstrate. You can never outgive.

h) **Always use the best tools**

As a handyman, your grandfather always bought the best tools. These tools would assist him in doing the best possible job. Whatever job or emergency arose at any time he was able to deal with it because he had the most up to date tools on the market. In business, the same principle applies. Those who use the best tools will always make quantum leaps if they put them to use.

So there you have some wise advice from an expert, your grandfather. Take note and apply these daily and be certain to win.

From one expert to another
Love you
Dad

THE 18TH LETTER

BeCoMe YoUr GrEaTeSt FaN

Applause rarely comes before an event. It is usually reserved for when battles have been fought and victories have been won. Ask any champion. This is why you must become your own cheerleader. You should in fact become your biggest fan.

Learn to tell yourself that you believe in yourself, that you respect your abilities and that you are proud to know yourself. You are the best. You are first class. You are dynamic. You are brilliant. You have what it takes.

It builds confidence. It increases stamina. It explodes potential within you. It drives you from where you are today to where you want to be in the future. It's the stuff of champions. Make the decision that you are going to do all that it takes to become the best you possibly can.

Children, within your head there are two voices. The first voice, and one that is so prevalent in millions of human minds, is the defeatist voice. This is the voice that says that someone else has more ability, or that someone else deserves a better deal than you do, or that someone else has more luck than you, or that someone else is better looking than you.

The other voice is the voice of the conqueror and of the

champion. It looks for your fine qualities and for your natural talents and abilities. It encourages you to grow stronger. It lifts and doesn't pull down. It builds up and doesn't destroy. It is willing to allow you to stretch your wings rather than clipping them. This voice leads you through the desert to find the oasis. This voice pulls you up the mountain until you have reached the peak. This voice helps you find that extra ounce of strength that will carry you across the line. It is the voice of the winner. You must tune your brain antennae into this voice, so that you can receive constant and clear reception.

♥

Before coming on duty, Detective Sergeant McPherson had dropped his wife off at the airport. She was visiting her mother. It was exactly twelve months since they'd tragically lost their only son in a boating accident. She wasn't finding it easy and it was often a challenge for him to get up to go to work. He had helped many people in his time but he didn't seem to be able to help his wife nor himself, for that matter.

An urgent call came over the radio, interrupting his train of thought. There was a reported break in at twenty-three St Bernard Court, Calapana. He and his partner were to investigate. It was 1.00 a.m. The caller had reported that there was a disturbance at the above address. However, when she was asked for her details, the woman immediately hung up.

This area was part of their normal patrol, so it was not too difficult to make a pass by of the residence. It wouldn't take long to see if there was anything suspicious happening at the reported address. These were the times in a police officer's life, when the adrenaline started to pump profusely through his body. This was the time when he had to listen to the positive side of his brain. There was no time to guess or wonder. It was in these moments that his confidence had to be operating at peak performance and when all his training had to come into play. He needed to be ready for anything or anybody. This was when courage ruled over fear and when his ability to instigate the element of surprise was paramount.

Arriving at number twenty-three, the detective noticed

that the front window was wide open and that the curtains were blowing freely in the coolness of the early morning breeze. No lights were on in the house and there was no noise to be heard coming from inside.

After parking the police car in front of the house, and dimming the car lights, both he and his partner hopped out to inspect the scene. The detective moved swiftly, yet quietly across the front lawn towards the open window; torch in one hand and gun in the other. He nodded to his partner to go around the back. The night was relatively quiet except for the occasional dog bark or the crow of a rooster whose time clock was malfunctioning.

Before arriving at the front window, he decided to turn his torch off. *'Nothing worse than becoming a moving target,'* he thought to himself. As quietly as he could, he stepped through the window that opened off the front porch and found himself in the main bedroom. Fortunately, there was sufficient light from the moon flooding through the side window, which allowed him to see some of the features of the room; a double bed, a dressing table, walk in robes and an ensuite off to the back of the room. Fairly neat and tidy, it looked as though nothing had been disturbed. There was no broken glass and no visible signs of forced entry.

He moved tentatively through the doorway and found himself staring down a hallway. This was a little harder to make out except for the fact that the skylight in the roof allowed some of the moonlight to filter into the room. It was a wooden polished floor with a long runner that stretched from the front door and right through to the kitchen.

He swiftly moved from room to room with his gun ever ready to counteract any surprise attack from the suspected intruder. As he did so, he could hear his partner systematically checking doors and windows at the back of the house.

With every room checked but one, he was feeling a little less nervous but from his experience it was no time to relax until every area had been covered. By this time, he had let his partner in the back door and they both, with eyes alert and guns at the ready, started their way down the stairwell, which led to the basement. The wooden steps unfortunately creaked with every move they made. His partner thought, *'If there's someone down here, we're goners.'*

They heard the scuttle of little feet moving swiftly down below. The detective whispered, *'Probably only a mouse.'* Evenso, their hearts still missed a beat. It was harder to see down here, so he tried to turn on his torch. To his disgust the light suddenly died. *'I knew I should have recharged those batteries yesterday,'* he mumbled under his breath. If his superiors ever found out about his careless oversight, he would really be in trouble.

They finally reached the bottom and with one shake of the detectives' torch the beam of light reappeared, allowing them to look into every nook and cranny of the basement. It was strewn with old bits of furniture and dozens of boxes covered in cobwebs and dust.

He noticed a yellow note pinned to the side of one of the boxes. The detective leaned over to read it. To his surprise, it was addressed to him.

Dear Detective Sergeant McPherson,

My name is Mimi Rogers. You helped me years ago when I had no home, by opening yours to me. I'll never forget your families' kindness. The thought of it has kept me going time and time again, even when the going's got rough. Well, I'm still toughing it out, trying to kick my drug habits.

I have something for you. I heard of your loss last year and I thought that you and your wife might have a place in your heart for this gift. By the time you get this note I will have long gone to start a new life. I'm sad yet happy that this gift will be left in your safe hands. I'll always be one of your greatest fans.

Mimi

He quickly opened the box and there inside, wrapped in a blanket, was a baby, fast asleep and at peace.

♥

If Mimi had learnt to be her own fan she may not have lived such a tragic life. So be your own fan. Be your greatest fan because you have what it takes to live a fantabulous life … yes, better than fantastic and much more than fabulous. Build your own pathway to adventure by focussing on your strengths, ignoring your critics (particularly the ones that come from within your own mind) and listen to the voice of the champion and the conqueror. Applaud your life as you rise to meet a new challenge, and greet each day as your friend. It has been created to take you one step further to the fulfilment of your desires and your dreams.

Every time I punch into the air with my fist and yell *'Yes'*, I suddenly feel that I have grown in stature on the inside. Whatever it takes, find your own special way to feel great about yourself and all the fine qualities that you have. Become a detective and discover the key that will unlock your door to your future. A dose of "positive" everyday will keep you growing and going and most importantly, be your biggest fan.

Love from one of your greatest fans
Dad

Step out of the maddening crowd, hang on to hope, draw on the dream and put everything you've got into what you believe.

THE 19TH LETTER

YoU aLrEaDy HaVe WhAt It TaKeS tO wIn

Many people are looking for the secret formula for success. Others are searching for the fastest way to get from where they are to where they want to go in life. They're always looking for some external program or formula that can carry them further towards the fulfilment of their dreams.

I did that for years. Armed with all this newly acquired information I decided that in my pursuit, I would have to delay my personal happiness: to some day in the far off distant future. In my search for what I felt was important, I decided that pain was going to have to be my chosen companion until all my dreams would finally come true.

Then I would hear speakers talking about *'enjoying the journey'*. That never made sense to me because as far as I was concerned, the journey that I was presently travelling was far from enjoyable. It was like asking someone who is sitting in a dentist chair and having a tooth drilled, to find the whole experience enjoyable. Surely, joy would only arrive long after the tooth was filled and the numbness had finally subsided. The repair process however was far from joyful. In addition, the repairing of a life was going to be a whole new and painful process.

After years of pain, I finally reached a point in my life where I decided to start enjoying the whole experience of building a successful life. I decided to become serious about not taking life too seriously. I discarded the lemon that was stuck between my lips and practiced bending the sides of those swollen lips upward on a more regular basis. So, even in the midst of the daily challenges and the stretching experiences that I was still facing, there started to be scatterings of joy and happiness. It made all the difference and proved a winning combination with those I lived with at home. It was a daily process and I had to keep working at it. I couldn't do it one day and then throw it away the next. It took constant work with consistent effort.

♥

So how do you turn life's challenges into a positive event? It has everything to do with attitude. One way to turn a negative attitude into a positive one is by first taking a stocktake of your life. The best way to find out where you're at is to first find out where you're at. I discovered that when I started to take a serious account of what I already had, I was to be pleasantly surprised. I found that I already had in my possession a lot of what I had been striving for.

Now, in no way do I want to downplay the importance of tape, CD or video programs and seminars because I buy them and attend them regularly myself. However, when the tape player is turned off and the crowds have dispersed from the latest seminar, that is the time when champions are born and battles are won. It's what happens when the doors are shut and you're all alone that will determine your future success. Use those tools as supplements but know this; you are already in possession of some fine resources that will form the basis of every success you experience in life.

In order to move forward in a positive direction and in a positive mindset, develop the habit of being thankful. Make a list of ten things that you can be thankful for right now. Here are my ten, by way of example. I could probably list a hundred but ten is a good start. These are straight off the top of my head as I write this letter to you.

Children, I'm thankful:

1. For fresh air to breathe
2. For you, my three children
3. For good health
4. For a clear mind
5. For fingers that enable me to type this letter
6. For my wife
7. For the view outside my study window
8. For the ability to be creative
9. For having the opportunity to put positive input into other peoples lives
10. For freedom of speech

Why don't you make your own list right now? You have a lot to be thankful for, just like me. Pick up a pen and make a list immediately.

1. _____

2. _____

3. _____

4. _____

5. _____

6. _____

7. _____

8. _____

9. _____

10. _____

It's all about being grateful. It's all about having a tank full of thankful. As one thankful person once said, if they wake up in the morning it has to be a great day. If they don't find their name in the obituaries, it has to be a fantastic day. Take a moment every day to be thankful. Take some time to tell someone else that you love them. Tell them that you are thankful that they're an important part of your life.

♥

As his children were preparing to leave for school, his youngest daughter sat on his knee and started to read from an old school book. These were short stories she had written in her school diary. Now with a middle name like 'Joy', I suppose that it was not surprising to find her stories filled with the following words … 'fun and love'. She simply enjoyed life and squeezed joy out of every moment with her laughter and her smile. She expressed thankfulness in a very demonstrative manner. When her dad did the smallest of things for her, for example when he had laminated a paper placemat that she had carefully decorated at school, it was as if he had presented her with a gold medallion. Every morning at the breakfast table her mat was religiously placed into position to catch any stray rice bubbles that might fall from her plate. She expressed her thankfulness with many hugs and many kisses.

♥

As adults, we need to constantly remind ourselves to hug and kiss life, no matter how it is presented to us. In all its imperfections there is always a seed of life to be found that we can be thankful for. Once we express our thanks for one facet of our complex life, we will soon discover yet another one.

Children, as you continue to move on into adulthood I'll give you this challenge. When was the last time you gave your husband or wife a really big hug and said that you loved them? How about your kids? When did you let your daughter cuddle up to you and when was the last time you looked at her, face to face, and said that you loved her? Hey dad, when did you grab hold of your son, no matter how big he is, and gave him a huge bear hug? Look at him eyeball to eyeball and say, *'I'm proud of you.'* Your children and partner are some of the greatest assets that you will ever have. Take time out to appreciate them and really tell them that you love them.

As you know, from time to time, I send you less formal letters. They are often little notes that say what I really feel about you. They always seem to find a prominent place in your bedrooms and stay there for weeks after the event. We have a lot to be thankful for and I'm thankful for you.

After you have made your thankful list, another one needs to follow. This is a list of all your talents. I dare you to try to list ten. What are you good at? What do you find easy to do? What do you enjoy doing? It doesn't have to specifically relate to work or to business. Just write them down. Some would call them your strengths. I want to call them the jewels of your life, the things that make you, you. Be proud of who you already are and what you are already in possession of. So go ahead; write down ten things that you are good at.

1. _____

2. _____

3. _____

4. _____

5. _____

6. _____

7. _____

8. _____

9. _____

10. _____

Now write down five qualities that you admire about yourself. Go on; blow your own trumpet.

1. _____

2. _____

3. _____

4. _____

5. _____

Here's a challenge. Email a family member, friend or associate and list five qualities that you admire about them. To help you get started note them below.

Name of person who is going to receive your
e (encouragement)-mail:

_____

The five qualities I admire in you are:

1. _____

2. _____

3. _____

4. _____

5. _____

Challenge them to then email someone else, not yourself, with a list of five qualities that they admire in one of their other friends. Imagine what can happen to our world if we could take time to do this. This encouragement can circumnavigate the globe in no time. It will give a whole new dimension to the letter 'e' in e-mail. Remember, 'e' stands for encouragement.

In a few lines, you have built some powerful ammunition that both you and your friends can draw upon whenever you hit a roadblock or need some reassurance.

You may even think of some other lists. Write them down, because you need to know that you are already in possession of some powerful winning qualities. These will take you from victory to victory and strength to strength. I really believe it.

I believe in you
Love Dad

*There are no
restrictions when the
power of belief
is released
in your life.*

THE 20TH LETTER

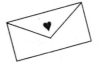

SlOw & sTeAdY: yOuR fAsT tRaCk To SuCcEsS

As a younger man I was convinced that the faster you drove yourself, the faster you would arrive at your destination. A great idea except for a few things. What if you don't have the necessary skills to guide your vehicle at that speed, whether it is a career or a business? What is fast and what is slow? What does one do with detours? Unfortunately, life is not always straightforward.

Let me encourage you to find your own pace, in time with your own timeclock and make it steady. Not stop, start, stop, and start. By consistent effort, you can gradually build into your life a momentum that will eventually carry you over the line and allow you to reach your goals. A constant hammering on one point will strengthen your determination to continue while at the same time weakening any resistance.

When Sir Edmund Hillary first failed to reach the summit of Mt Everest he spoke to the mountain and declared that it was never going to get any bigger but that he was. History records how this man, who became bigger and more determined on the inside, conquered the heights of the tallest mountain on planet earth.

Satisfaction comes from running your own race and by learning to beat your best by becoming better. Sure, we are in a competitive world, but to achieve the greatest sense of peace and achievement, it is best to run in your own lane. Seek ways to encourage those who are running their race while you push ahead in the pursuit of your own personal goals.

♥

When we moved north to Queensland, I had daily access to a large pool. Now because of the warmer climate I made the decision that I was going to strengthen my swimming skills.

As a child, I was not a strong swimmer and because of that, I had some frightening experiences in water. I recall the time I nearly drowned at a swimming carnival in the middle of a twenty-five-metre race. Then there was the time I was dumped in the surf. The huge waves tumbled me over and over and over across the bottom of the ocean floor until I finally bobbed up to the top like a cork, gasping for air.

I had attended swimming lessons a number of times throughout my childhood but whatever information they put into my head was never transferred to my body. My major challenge was learning how to breathe correctly. Whenever I would try to do freestyle, I would continually run out of breath.

However, with a few tips from you and your mother, I set out to become an excellent swimmer by taking time every day to swim laps in the pool. I soon noticed that I was getting stronger and stronger. You were my best teachers, because you taught me simple concepts that I could easily understand. It wasn't long before my breathing was improving and I was starting to glide effortlessly back and forth across the pool. I had never done this before in my whole life. I was no longer running out of breath. I was no longer huffing and puffing with every lap. I was no longer getting physically tired in both my arms and my legs. Even my speed was increasing and my confidence was soaring. My body strength was growing daily in my arms, shoulders and my torso.

Swimming is no longer a painful experience but has in fact become a joy. Slowly and steadily, mastery has been effected through practice and the occasional tuition.

♥

Mastery can take place in any area of your life: whether it is learning a new instrument, or conducting a new business, in playing a chosen sport or in learning a foreign language. The important thing though is to allow yourself time to achieve. Everybody's pace is different and comparing yourself with another human being's performance can be the very thing that will rob you of the joy of your own personal achievement.

Keep your eyes firmly fixed on the vision that you have for your own life and you will find that you'll start to hit the bullseye more often. The bullseye is the fulfilment of your goal and the pinnacle of your achievement. A successful life first sees and then does. A steady eye takes you from where you are to where you want to be in the future. For although at times the journey seems too slow you are building towards exponential growth. At first, the curve starts its rise ever so slightly but with each tap from your pick, as it shapes and moulds the sculptured life that you are creating for yourself, the curve is starting to rise. It's starting to build. It's starting to grow and the rate of increase is moving forward with each breath that you breathe, each positive move that you make, and each step that you take.

Although none of us is freed from facing difficulty and opposition in our lives, we can choose to use them as our building blocks along success road. Our obstacles become our stepping stones to victory.

♥

A man set off on a very long journey. He had set out in search of a land that promised to be all that he had wished for and desired. He had been told that in this new land there was much opportunity and much gold. It was said that in this land he would find wealth and respect. Therefore, after kissing his family goodbye he left with all his possessions on his donkey.

He was in search of his future and knew that he would find it.

After many days of travelling through rain, hail and shine, he came upon a mountain of rocks that spread as far as the eye could see. He had never imagined that in order to reach his destination, he would have to face such an inimitable obstacle. There was a sign on the side of the road which said, *'Those who pull down will be those who build.'*

Now many a traveller had passed this way before and many had read this sign. Most had been discouraged by the mountain and had turned back. Others had tried to find a way around the mountainous pile of rocks but had perished. Some had even tried to climb it, to their own peril, because the rocks would slip, slide, and create an avalanche.

So as he pondered at the foot of the mountain, he thought to himself, *'Although I want to get to the land where there is a promise of great riches, I realize that if I'm ever going to get there I must first do what I'm instructed to do.'*

He camped at the foot of the mountain and decided that if he was going to move the mountainous pile of rocks he might as well find a use for them. So, he set up a stall on the side of the road and sold pieces of the dug up rock to tourists who passed by. He found that the more he dug the more beautiful the rocks became; many and varied in shape and colour. People liked the coloured rocks and bought them as treasures to give to friends and relatives as gifts.

He built himself a home beside the mountain of rocks and was soon joined by his family. After living in this house for twelve months, he found that his house was cool in the summer months and warm in the winter. Inspired by this discovery, he transported the rocks to neighbouring towns and people began then to build their homes. In the past, the people had only ever built their houses out of wood. He then took some of the softer rocks, crushed them and hired others to work for him. The crushed rocks were then sold to owners of those new stone homes as gravel for their walkways and as paving for the many roads that now led to the mountain.

Slowly and steadily, he systematically dismantled the mountain. The more he dug, the more he realized that the riches he had sought had been found in solving the problem that he had faced along the way. In helping others, he had in fact helped himself. To his own surprise, what had once been an obstacle had become his greatest asset. What had seemed as a detour had become his delight.

His advice to all that travelled this road was, *'Stop a while. Slow down and steady yourself to have a closer look. Success may already be in your hands. Your obstacle could just be the opportunity you've been looking for.'*

Love to see you win
Dad

The more you give,
the more you get
to give again.

THE 21ST LETTER

Be BeTtEr

A farmer had a stubborn mule. It would never do anything that he instructed it to do. While reading a newspaper one day he came across an ad which read, *'Mule trainer - we train your mule with love'.* Now being a peace loving man, he thought to himself, *'This is exactly the type of person I want to train my mule.'* So he rang the trainer and organized an appointment. When the day finally arrived and the trainer was formally introduced to the mule, he proceeded to walk around the animal before picking up a large piece of wood. *'I wonder what he's going to do with that?'* the farmer thought. Before he could blink, the trainer had hit the mule over the head and the animal had fallen flat on its face in the dirt. The owner yelled, *'What'd you do that for? I thought you trained them with love.'* The trainer responded, *'I do, but first I've got to get their attention.'*

♥

Now that I have caught your attention, we can continue with the next letter. Throughout my lifetime, I have learnt a great deal about what it takes to live a successful life. I have also learnt that not only should we strive for success, but that we should strive for significance. Everything I learn becomes so much more significant when I share it with someone else. Success is to be shared with others by encouraging them to never settle for less than their best.

Success should always be seen as our own personal challenge to dig deep, to find what our strengths are, and then to develop them. Success is the willingness to fail until we win. It is the ability to face rejection and know that rejection can be the pathway to victory. You were never created to imitate others, but to learn from others and their success, and to then discover and develop your own unique formula.

Someone once said that in order to be successful, you must find out what you like doing and then find someone to pay you for doing it. Compete against your own ability and against your last effort. Make it your goal to get better. Make every step an excellent step and begin to dream even bigger dreams as you choose to live life to the fullest. It's all about seeking to do better, to be better and to achieve better results.

Following are six points built around the word 'better'. It is only as we seek to do better that we will become better people and create a better world.

Beat your last effort. Always look for a better way to do something; whether it is the way you type a letter, build a house, manage your staff or the way you promote and sell your service or merchandise. Keep alert to all that is going on around you and take what's good and make it your own. Sam Walton, who was at one time the richest man in America, would visit his competition in the retail industry. While other members of his staff were wondering why he should bother, because he was already the biggest and the best, he would always find something that someone else was doing better. He would adapt it immediately and put it into action in his own stores. We can all get better.

Explain what you have learnt to someone else. Things I have learnt best and remember best are the things I have taught to someone else. If you're talented in a particular area, teach someone else what you know. Teach your own children. Even as children you are ready to learn principles which will stay with you for the rest of your days.

I remember the first cake sale conducted by my eldest daughter. Chocolate cake was taken from door to door in our street. She organized and designed her own advertising campaign on a sheet of paper. This was held by one of her hired helps. Soon many of the children in the street surrounded her and when anyone opened their front door, a crowd confronted them. She had to decide on the correct price structure, verify that her marketing technique was correct and that her sale spiel was well prepared. The product was checked for quality by the lick of a finger and before long she returned home with a pocketful of money and no cakes. She had one complaint though. She went on to explain that before she had started the venture she had agreed to a partnership with one of the neighbours - the one who had held the paper sign. As a direct result of this agreement, she had to split the profit 50/50. *'Next time,'* she said, *'I'll do it differently.'* A lesson learnt. From her experience, she is now better able to instruct her younger brother and sister.

♥

Trust Your Strengths. There is an element of risk involved when you begin to trust your talents and your abilities. Take time out to take stock of your strengths and note your weaknesses. Major on your strengths and delegate your weaknesses.

♥

A young cricket player was endeavouring to impress his new coach by showing how he could be an all-rounder. He could bowl fast, he could spin and even throw down a few medium pace balls. Then he would pad up ready to bat. There was no doubt in the mind of the coach that this fellow would go far with a cricketing career.

The coach came up to the young player after the practice session and asked, *'Of all your abilities in cricket, which one is the best?'*

He replied, *'Well my best bowl is the spin, then the fast ball with an inswinger and finally the medium pace. I can also bat pretty well.'*

'So what have you been majoring on?' asked the coach.

'I've been trying to improve my inswinger and my medium pace. If I can improve those, I should have a great season.'

'I don't mind you batting,' added the coach. *'I'll place you in the middle order, but with your bowling, from watching you, your best bowl is your spin. Spend most of each practice session developing your spin with a very occasional faster delivery and you'll help the team win most of their games.'*

That's exactly what he did and by the end of the season not only had the team won the competition but he was voted the best player of the year.

Try Again, even if you have failed before. You have probably heard the well-repeated saying that we must fail our way to success. Could you ever see yourself telling a baby, who is desperately trying to learn to walk, to stop trying because he's failed repeatedly? No! Well it is no different to learning to live a successful life. Life is not just a road to success but should in fact be called a road of success. We should never stop learning how to succeed until the day that we die.

The Author James Michener has been an inspiration to me, particularly when I read his autobiography, *'The World is my Home.'* His first book wasn't published until he was forty years old and then he went on to have an extremely successful career well into his nineties. What I liked about him was that there were times in his career when he wanted to write what he wanted to write and not necessarily what his publishers wanted to publish. One book was on Japanese art. His publishers wouldn't touch it, so he published it himself. It became a bestseller in Japan. He tried and succeeded.

Energize yourself daily. Every day we need a recharge of the motivational batteries. To become a better writer I must become a better reader. If we are to achieve great things in this life, we need a regular diet of positive and uplifting material. There is an abundance of material in the market place to feed us. Buy it and inwardly digest it on a daily basis.

Reach Higher. In order to reach higher we are going to have to stretch further than we've stretched before. It has everything to do with becoming better and if we are to overcome stagnation and mediocrity, we are, at some point, going to have to step out from the masses and determine to do things a little differently. Did you know that only 1 to 5% of the population ever reach retirement age financially successful and independently wealthy? That means that only a very small percentage has ever reached higher in the financial realm. However, there is so much more that we can reach for ... career satisfaction, healthy family relationships, marital stability etc. Decide what you want and then find a way to get it honestly. Write your dream down and then get to work to seeing it fulfiled.

So, all in all children; make it your goal to get better. Never settle for less than your best. If we can all get better in even the smallest way possible we will make a better world, run better businesses, have healthier bank accounts and maintain better relationships. In the whole process, we will become a much, much better person.

I am better for loving you
Dad

*Your greatest
investment?
Plant a little seed
of love into
someone's life.*

THE 22ND LETTER

LoVe LoTs

The most powerful ingredient in any relationship is love. Lots of it. Nothing longstanding is ever built on the foundations of hate. This has been clearly evident as we take a quick flick through the pages of history. The Empires produced by a number of dictators, even throughout this last century, lasted for only a season. Ultimately the mortar of hate that held their reign together crumbled. To this day we see not only their ruins but in more recent cases, the scars in the lives of those touched by their destructive rule.

You can never love enough and you can always love a little bit more. Always take time out to express it in both word and/or deed. I have touched on this in my previous writings. However, because I feel this is such an important point it needs to be raised again.

When you show love towards someone else, you are showing him or her the highest form of respect. You must love your customers, love your clients, love your business associates, love your suppliers, love your employees, love those whom you work alongside and if you work for someone else, then even love your boss.

How does one demonstrate love, you may ask? Well let me tell you an ancient story that demonstrates what I perceive as one of the finest examples of love shown by a father to his son.

♥

A father had two sons and the younger one demanded that his father should give him his share of the estate. He didn't want to wait until his father was dead before receiving his inheritance. He wanted to experience a living will. So the father divided his property and gave his youngest son his share.

It wasn't long after this that the young son gathered all his gear together, packed up and set off for a distant land. While he was there, he squandered all his inheritance in wild and raucous living.

A severe famine hit the land and he found himself in a desperate situation. In order to eat, he hired himself out to a farmer who sent him into his field to feed the pigs. He was so hungry that all he wanted to do was to join the pigs as they fed on the pods that he scattered amongst them.

When he finally came to his senses, he realized that while he was literally dying of hunger his father's servants were eating and living better than he was.

That's when he made a quality decision. He would leave immediately and return to his father. He would tell him that he had been wrong and that he was no longer worthy to be called a son. He would ask to be allowed to live in his house as a servant. So the son left and returned home.

While he was still a long way off, the father saw him and felt sorry for him. He quickly came down, ran towards him, hugged him, and kissed him.

The son dropped to his knees before his father and said, *'Father I have not only hurt you but I have in fact dishonoured God. I'm not worthy to be called your son.'* However, the father said to his servants, *'Quickly! Bring me the best clothing and dress him. Put jewellery on him, put shoes on his feet, and prepare a homecoming feast for my son. Let's celebrate, for I thought that my son was lost forever, but look, he has returned.'*

♥

It's easy to love someone who returns your love. However,

to be the one who keeps handing out the love while being on the receiving end of another's unloveliness is where love really shines. To keep loving when all you receive is rejection. That is the key. Therein lies the power. To forgive and to forget. To hold no grudges. To harbour no jealousy or envy. To keep short accounts with those whom you do business with. To forget wrongs and to overlook shortcomings. To encourage when discouraged. To lift when put down. To give when there's seemingly nothing left to give. To walk the extra mile and to show the extra smile. To speak kind and uplifting words. These are the outworkings of true love.

Even while the son was squandering his inheritance in a far off land, the father never stopped loving his son. I would imagine that every evening he would sit out on his front porch, looking and longing for his young son to return along the road that he had left. He never gave up on his youngest. No matter how negative the situation seemed, no matter how many days passed without even a postcard from his son, he waited and was ready to embrace him and to accept him for who he was and not for what he had done. All mistakes were washed clean. His slate was clear in his father's eyes. He was reinstated and I would imagine that from that day there was no mention of the mistakes that had been made or the fortune that had been squandered. In the eyes of the father his most precious possession had returned, his son.

♥

Can we look at the unlovely and see beneath the exterior to discover a jewel? Can we dig beneath the veneer that so many humans hide behind, in order to find the potential that lies within? Can we pause a moment and listen to one who maybe comes from a different town or a different socio-economic background and enjoy their company? For it is not the packaging that is of prime importance. Some people's gifts need to be unwrapped before they can begin to shine. An expression of love from you could be the very key that will release the potential that lies within that precious life.

I recently sent a love letter to a friend. I hadn't seen him in years but my mother had fortunately bumped into his wife in

Sydney. When she told me of this I was warmly reminded of the beautiful investment this man had put into my own life many years ago. Here's a portion of a letter that I sent to him with a copy of one of my books. He was one of those special people who invested lots of love in my young life and I just wanted to share with him how grateful I was. It was now my chance to send a little dose of love back in his direction …

Good Morning Tom!

You might find this letter somewhat of a surprise. A blast from the past as it were. Clare apparently met up with my mum a little while ago and consequently she was mentioning the fact with me recently. The mention of your name flooded back a whole set of wonderful memories.

Please find enclosed a copy of one of my books, which I would like to give to both Clare and yourself as a gift this Christmas. It is in appreciation for the time that you took out of your busy schedule to help me as a child with my maths, for teaching me how to construct a speech and for barracking for me at those soccer games, many years ago. Your expression of interest in this young life will always be dear to my heart and for that, I thank you. To Clare, I also thank you for lending your husband to me at those times …

… Anyway, I just wanted to let you know that the seeds you planted into my life were good seed and that we are all benefiting from the crop that was and is still being produced.

May God continue to bless you in your life and ministry.

Take time to plant a little seed of love into someone's life today. It will be the greatest investment that you can ever make in your whole life.

Lots and lots of love
Dad

THE 23RD LETTER

PuSh AhEaD wItH pErSiStEnCy

The door of opportunity has the word 'push' permanently carved on one side of the door. The world doesn't always arrange for things to simply fall into our lap. Remember, to become an overnight success it usually takes about fifteen years.

Children, it has been my turn to look after you this morning while your mum was out. You've been on school holidays, so from time to time you like to visit dad and see how he's going with his next creation. It was interesting to note that I was having to inject a fresh dose of persistence to proceed with this, the 23rd Letter, when you, my son came in, put your arms around my shoulder and asked, *'How's it going dad?'*

Still deep in thought, I turned and responded, *'I'm up to the 23rd letter.'*

'Wow!' you exclaimed, *'and how many more do you have to write to finish?'*

'Seven more.'

The next few words were exactly what I needed. *'Congratulations Dad! That's really great.'* Thanks son.

A few simple words spoken in season always spur me on. They help me to persist until a job is completed and a task is well done. You quickly left the room and proceeded to herald the good news throughout the whole household. It wasn't long before your younger sister burst into the room. While taking a good look at what was written on the computer screen she suddenly exploded, *'Congratulations Dad!'* I'm not sure if she fully understood what she was congratulating me about but two doses of that sort of medicine on one day is good for anybody's soul. Thanks baby.

♥

When I think of persistence, I think of the game of golf. As I recently watched a golf tournament, it was evident that the persistent ones were the ones who would ultimately take out the winner's crown.

As a child, I was fortunate enough to live just up the road from the local golf course. I had been given a golf set by my mother's stepfather and would from time to time play either with my dad or with a friend. For many years, the golf course was only nine holes. The other nine holes were being prepared with landfill from the local rubbish tip and it was many years before it was a full-fledged course.

The second hole was my favourite because the tee off was situated high above the treeline, while the green was way down at the bottom of a hill. Being a par 3, I would often achieve it, even as a child.

It is an incredible sensation when you connect well with a golf ball. However, when you misdirect one, that is when persistence has to kick in. First, you have to find the ball and it was always amazing how in most cases I would find two or three other balls but could never locate mine.

Golf is a game of such diverse action. At the tee off you have to hit that little white ball with all your might but on arriving at the green you have to hold back on that strength and use restrained and directed force to sink it into the cup.

I loved the long fairways; I could really get my teeth into not just the first shot but a couple of other shots, using a number of different irons to achieve the desired result. The thing I loved about the golf course was the fact that it was such a peaceful place. It was a little white ball, nature and just me. That is, unless someone was getting upset over a bungled shot.

In order to achieve the best possible score I had to be persistent, right up until the final green. There was no time to relax because with every missed stroke or lost ball there was an ultimate penalty. This would be evident in the final tallied score.

Real life is so much like a game of golf. Both have a starting point and an end. In between there are the misdirected hits, the very occasional hole in ones, the encounters with the sand traps and water. There are periods where we have to fight our way out of the rough. There are times when we need to swing with all our might and then there are other times when we need to quietly and confidently sink another putt. It requires the much-needed focus on the current goal. After achieving that, another one is quickly set before us.

When a shot lands us in a very difficult situation behind a clump of trees, our view of the up and coming green is blocked. We have a choice. We can choose either a penalty shot or make the best of a bad situation by swinging with all our might, while hoping for the best. The important thing is that we get back onto the fairway. Life isn't always fair either and it's what we do with the 'unfairway' (that's a word I just decided to invent) that will separate us from the rest of the clubhouse.

When I watch champion golfers playing, I love to watch how they fight back from a sandtrap shot or from some other particularly hard situation. I love watching them get over the last bogeyed hole and then take on the next hole to get a birdie or even an eagle. It is as if the last disaster never happened; that the past never existed and that the only thing that needs to be concentrated on is the here and now.

This is a powerful lesson for all of us. Instead of carrying around the garbage from the past and allowing it to trip us up, we should forget it and simply move on to achieve the here and now goal.

Now, I am all for having long term goals, but it is the achievement of the short term goals and the total focus on doing what is important today that will ultimately enable you to fulfil your life goal. This will also help you in achieving your best result.

Obviously, for any golfer to achieve his or her optimum ability, there needs to be the injection of consistent practice, the advice of a coach and the tenacity to pursue the best possible score. Winners require a persistent and consistent performance, day in and day out. It doesn't matter whether there is wind, rain or sunshine. Whatever the lay of the land is like and whatever the size of the greens or how many dips and curves there may be, experienced golfers are focussed on only one thing and that is to improve on their last score.

A golfer doesn't, on a bad day, decide to leave the golf course on the twelfth hole because there is too much wind or it's too hot or because he has already made a number of misdirected hits. No, he keeps on until the eighteenth. The game is not over until he has completed the whole course. If it's a major tournament, the golfer may be required to come back to the same course on four consecutive days. No, a golfer needs to forget what has gone before, whether it is good, bad or ugly and then take on each fresh hole with a fresh attitude.

So, think of your life as a game of golf. Each day is the opportunity to hit a perfect drive down the next fairway of your life. It is yet another chance to sink that perfect putt or to make that beautiful and precise wedge shot. More divots, but yet more progress as you hit yet another par and maybe even achieve the ultimate in a hole in one. They do happen and why not you? It's another day to take a closer look at your daily goals and to set out to reach them. Every hole completed is another step closer to the fulfilment of your persistent life. Make every shot count and don't waste one along the way.

Driven by love — Dad

THE 24TH LETTER

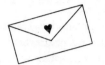

EmBaRk On A mIsSiOn

The good news about being a winner is that in order to win you don't have to be able to hit every single ball that comes your way.

There is often a misconception in the community, which says that in order to be a winner you need to be the one who hits a home run each and every time. But in reality there are very few human beings who can consistently turn out those sort of averages. In any mission undertaken by man, woman or child there will be times when you will miss. The difference between those who win and those who lose is quite simple. Winners keep hitting until they hit more than they miss. Loser's quit. It's interesting to take a quick look at the word mission and find out that the first four letters actually spell "miss".

I remember hearing a salesman tell me that the reason he sold more products than the other sales staff on the sales floor was because he talked to more people. While the others were standing around deciding whether the person who walked through the front door was going to buy or not, he was already talking to them. He made many misses but because of his constant performance in stepping up to the plate, he hit more home runs.

♥

There were a few car salesmen standing around. They sold expensive cars. It was a Friday afternoon and things had been a bit slow and everyone was just about ready to go home when a very ill dressed man stumbled in the front door. He was unshaven and the smell of him drifted across the room to where the salesmen were standing. The three salesmen had a quick chat amongst themselves. The youngest was nominated to go and serve the customer as the more experienced salesmen said, *'Talk to him then get rid of him.'*

The young salesman decided that although this gentleman didn't look anything like the other exclusive clients that they normally dealt with, he would at least treat the man with some respect. After talking to the scruffily dressed elderly man for a while, the young salesman soon discovered that beneath that exterior there was someone who was quite intelligent. After discussing in detail the features of the Rolls Royce with the prospective client and establishing a price for the vehicle, the old man pulled out his cheque book from beneath his overcoat and wrote a cheque for the full amount. He handed both his cheque and his banker's business card to the young man and said that he would be in first thing Monday morning to pick up the car. The young man, still recovering from shock, watched as the man turned and shuffled out the front door.

Still coming to grips with what had just happened, he walked into his boss's office, where all the other salesmen were now sitting, sipping cups of coffee.

He exploded, *'Guess what?'*

'What?'

'I just sold the Rolls.'

One of the salesmen, who had suggested that the young man should be the one to see the tramp, nearly dropped his coffee as he spluttered, *'What?'*

'I just sold the Rolls. He'll be in on Monday to pick it up. Here's

his cheque. I'll just go and give his bank manager a call.'

'It's probably a rubber cheque,' one of the other salesmen snidely remarked. *'He couldn't possibly have that sort of money.'*

When Monday arrived, so too did the buyer. However, this time he was dressed in a three-piece suit and was cleanly shaven. On receiving the keys to his new vehicle he handed five crisp hundred dollar bills over to the young salesman saying, *'You'll go a long way young man if you always remember to never judge a book by it's cover. Whenever I do my poverty act, I always end up getting the best salesman. You are one of the elite in your field. Well done! When I need another car I'll come and see you.'* With that he drove off, while the other salesmen looked on in envy.

♥

The young salesman was a winner and your mission is to become a winner on a consistent basis. So what makes a winner? Here are 100 winning points that illustrate what I call my 'Portrait of a Winner'. See how many of these are operating in your life. If you can answer yes to between 1 and 50 then you are a winner with great potential. If you get between 51 and 75, you are a winner who is starting to really use your winning potential. If you get between 76 and 100, you are a winner.

The following chart is divided up into four parts. Complete all four and add up your total.

Section A: Tick if your answer is YES
1. I am not afraid of making mistakes .... ❑
2. I am willing to take a chance .... ❑
3. I am always looking for ways to do something better .. ❑
4. I forget the failures of the past and look at
        each new day through fresh eyes .... ❑
5. I invest in my own personal development .... ❑
6. I am never afraid to discard a non-producing
        idea in order to start afresh .... ❑
7. I smile even when I don't feel like smiling .... ❑
8. I laugh in the face of disaster .... ❑
9. I speak positive words .... ❑

10. If I have nothing good to say,
    I keep my mouth shut .... ☐
11. I have the winning habit of reading every day .... ☐
12. I listen to instructional tapes on a regular basis .... ☐
13. I finish what I start .... ☐
14. I delegate .... ☐
15. I exercise my body as well as my mind .... ☐
16. I have the mind of a student .... ☐
17. I recognize and applaud other winners .... ☐
18. I look for solutions, not problems .... ☐
19. I never criticize .... ☐
20. I know how to forgive .... ☐
21. I write lots of notes .... ☐
22. I give lots of hugs .... ☐
23. I make *'I love you'* a big part of my vocabulary .... ☐
24. I am not afraid of saying, *'I was wrong'* .... ☐
25. I return telephone calls .... ☐

Total out of 25 = _____

Section B: <u>Tick if your answer is YES</u>

1. I'm a good listener .... ☐
2. I am a giver .... ☐
3. I am a believer in myself as well as others .... ☐
4. I give a strong handshake .... ☐
5. I save and invest for the future .... ☐
6. I step out where others fear to tread .... ☐
7. I look other people in the eye during conversations ..... ☐
8. I walk tall and have good posture .... ☐
9. I work hard and smart and play hard and smart .... ☐
10. I encourage others to be the best they can be .... ☐
11. I look for good in others .... ☐
12. I create opportunity .... ☐
13. I speak the future into reality .... ☐
14. I am confident .... ☐
15. I am secure in my personality .... ☐
16. I reach beyond my comfort zone .... ☐
17. I reward myself for even little achievements .... ☐
18. I am a goal setter .... ☐

19. I write my goals ☐
20. I refer to my goals regularly ☐
21. I am always writing down new goals ☐
22. I exhort others to pursue their goals ☐
23. I don't seek out other people's applause ☐
24. I walk the extra mile ☐
25. I am an initiator ☐

Total out of 25 = _____

Section C: Tick if your answer is YES
1. I see a rainbow for every storm ☐
2. I would rather win a friend than win an argument ☐
3. I am not status conscious ☐
4. I am all things to all people ☐
5. I walk the talk ☐
6. I keep my word ☐
7. I am punctual ☐
8. I am reliable ☐
9. I am trustworthy ☐
10. I am happy to help ☐
11. I am polite and courteous ☐
12. I take care with the way I dress ☐
13. I keep my shoes clean ☐
14. I keep my hair neatly trimmed ☐
15. I am orderly ☐
16. I use a diary ☐
17. I answer the telephone in a professional manner ☐
18. I think of others first ☐
19. I say *'thank you'* and *'please'* on a consistent basis ☐
20. I build others up and don't pull them down ☐
21. I meet with other winners on a regular basis ☐
22. I never quit but may from time to time
        adjust my swing ☐
23. I am persistent ☐
24. I am compassionate ☐
25. I have a passion for life ☐

Total out of 25 = _____

Section D: Tick if your answer is YES

1. I share what I have with others .... ☐
2. I take time out to talk to a child .... ☐
3. I like people .... ☐
4. I treat my own body with respect .... ☐
5. I show respect to others .... ☐
6. I never say never .... ☐
7. I swim upstream .... ☐
8. I am a non-conformist .... ☐
9. I get things done .... ☐
10. I have conviction .... ☐
11. I try .... ☐
12. I seize opportunity .... ☐
13. I embrace change and make it my friend .... ☐
14. I am always taking action .... ☐
15. I run towards a challenge .... ☐
16. I know that through stretching beyond
    my ability I will grow .... ☐
17. I do what it takes to get a job done .... ☐
18. I either follow a system or invent my own .... ☐
19. I lead by example .... ☐
20. I know that when the dream is big
    then that's all that counts .... ☐
21. I know that one of life's greatest teachers is experience . ☐
22. I have a mentor .... ☐
23. I have strong values .... ☐
24. I am well informed .... ☐
25. I am on a mission to make this world
    a better place for all of us to live in .... ☐

Total out of 25 = _____

My overall score was: Section A: _____ + Section B: _____
+ Section C: _____ + Section D: _____
Total A B C D = _____

How did you go? What was your score out of 100? Make winning your mission in life and as you win, help others to win as well.

Mission Possible - Love Dad

THE 25TH LETTER

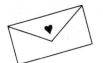

MoVe WiTh ThE tImEs

All the onlookers moved to each side of the walkway as they watched a very unusual sight. Here was a marathon runner, dressed in all the appropriate gear; lightweight shorts and singlet with sports socks and running shoes on his feet. However, the most unusual thing about him was that up and down both of his arms he was wearing dozens of watches. There were gold ones and silver ones, digital ones and Swiss ones. In fact every conceivable type of watch, including one with the face of Mickey Mouse. Beads of sweat gathered around each one as he pounded down the pavement.

When asked what he was doing, he simply smiled as he answered, *'I'm just moving with the times.'*

♥

We must move with the times because life never stands still. Those who try to resist or hold back from change will either be run over or be left far behind.

Children, I desire that you remain at the cutting edge of life and of all the experiences it will offer you throughout your lifetime. I want you to be constantly open to new ideas and developments in whatever field you choose to follow. I want to encourage you to always wear the hat of a student. I want you to continue to be excited about learning new and better ways to approach the challenges that face each new generation.

What if IBM had stuck with the Golfball electric typewriter? What if McDonalds had failed to reduce the amount of waste produced by their Styrofoam packaging? What if record companies refused to accept the changes imposed by the introduction of the compact disc and now the Digital Video Disk. DVD is even set to outstrip the Compact Disk Read-Only Memory or CD-ROM. What if the horse and buggy had been favoured more than the motor vehicle or sea travel rather than aeroplanes? What if the railways wouldn't move aside for the semi- trailers?

Just in the past forty years, there have been incredible leaps and bounds in the area of new developments. Let me cite just a few. Skateboards, silicon chips that contain thousands of integrated circuit components within a few millimetres. The photocopying machine. Aluminium drinking cans to replace glass bottles. Heart replacement valves, communication satellites, cassette tapes, the video recorder, vitamin C, the jumbo jet, the floppy disk, the Concorde, pocket calculators, the personal computer, the Walkman, the Space shuttle, the computer mouse, genetic fingerprinting, the Pentium chip that contains 3.1 million transistors and has a capacity of 100 MIPS making it able to process 100 million instructions per second. These are just a few of the millions of changes that have occurred in our world in the last forty years.

What can we expect in the next forty years? We live in a generation where we have watched man walk on the surface of the moon. We have seen images sent back to us from places as far as Mars and Jupiter. We have even travelled into the depths of the human anatomy to see the inner workings of the machine that keeps us moving. When a new product is released into the market place we hear reports of yet a better one that has already superseded the former.

However, with all these superficial developments happening around us, how can we best prepare ourselves to face the incredibly fast paced changes that will bombard our world both today and tomorrow?

Let me present to you just a few suggestions based around the word TECHNOLOGY:

Take time to learn: You should be spending at least twenty to thirty minutes a day learning about something new, whether it is information accessed off the Internet, from a book, a magazine, a tape, video or CD or from attending a seminar or listening to an educational radio or television program. This is vital to keep your mind alert and current. There are so many opportunities in our world today to learn about new ways or methods. Grab the opportunity and make it a consistent habit.

Experiment with new methods: Not every new method or every new idea will necessarily produce results but at least take time to experiment with it. See if it can add an extra positive dimension to your life. Before you reject anything, test it. You may be pleasantly surprised. Where a prepared mind meets an opportunity there is success.

Collect new information: When it comes to new technology and new ideas, become like a bowerbird. A bowerbird loves to collect and return with his new discoveries to the nesting place. Your nesting place is your brain. Gather information, take notes, cut out paper and magazine clippings, then file them. It may just be the information you will be looking for down the track. Keep a journal; take notes in your diary, record them in a file on your computer and as you store more of this information it may be something that can be used in the future. Become a good collector.

Help others by sharing what you know: Don't be a Mr or Mrs Scrooge. Once you have discovered new information, find someone to share it with. It may be in a discussion over a cup of coffee or in a letter or a note. Suggest a good book or magazine that you believe would be of value to them. Having been the student of research, become the teacher, even if it's in an informal setting. You don't have to have a classroom to be a teacher. All you need is one student. The world is full of students and they are always on the look out for a teacher who is willing to share their knowledge with them.

Never reject anything until you have the full picture: Too many people, too soon, cast out an idea before it has had a chance to go under the microscope. Remember that great ideas are either coming towards you or passing you by. So always keep a notebook handy to write any new ideas down before they disappear again. Then take the time to check it out. If you still think it worthy of your attention, go for it.

Openly accept new input: With a spirit of openness, you are always going to come off best. This doesn't mean that you should swallow everything you see or hear. Having an open mind though will ward off the onset of mental rigor mortis or vision arthritis. There's nothing worse than coming across young people who have stopped thinking.

Look for a better way: Improve your chances of ongoing success by always keeping up with the changes happening in our society. There is plenty of information on the Internet. By flicking through magazines, it will keep you in touch with what is happening in our world. Read on a regular basis and keep your ears and eyes open for fresh information. We live in the age of ever increasing information technology, so use it. Ride the wave of change; don't resist it but allow yourself to flow with it. Always ask, is there a better way I can do this to get a better result?

Organise your thoughts: My journal, along with my diary, allows me to keep my thoughts in order. They also allow me to express myself in a format that can be used as a ready reference at a later date. It's for my eyes only. In addition, I have a filing system where I store any new information. New ideas are committed to paper so that I'm then free to move on to the next thought. Keep a pen and pad handy next to your bed. Some great ideas appear in the middle of the night.

Give any new method a chance to develop: Time tells us a lot about any new idea. Some of the greatest ideas ever developed have taken years to fulfil their hidden potential. If you think it's worthy of your attention, stick with it.

You have the ability to turn this information to your advantage: Belief in yourself is of prime importance if you're going to be in step with the changes that are happening in our world today. Believe in your ability to learn, believe in your ability to adapt, believe in your capacity to take on board a whole swag of new information. Remember that even when you become advanced in years, you can teach old dogs new tricks. It's all to do with your state of mind.

So like the man with the many watches, move with the times and ride the crest of every new wave. Those who do will swim and not sink.

Got my floaties on and I'm ready to jetski ...
Love Dad

*Winners keep
hitting until they
hit more than
they miss.
Losers quit.*

THE 26TH LETTER

GeT eXcItEd

There was a roar from the crowd as the entertainer finished her last number for the evening's performance. It had been a wonderful night as she played all her hits. The air was electric. People were standing in their seats. Others were dancing up and down the aisles. The clapping thundered throughout the auditorium, and at times, the yelling and the screams of delight drowned out even the music as it pounded out of the huge speakers, that were suspended from the ceilings rafters.

She only had time to grab a glass of cool and refreshing water before her bodyguards ushered her back onto the stage for the encore. As the spotlight unveiled her presence on the stage, the noise suddenly exploded again and moved in waves back and forth across the room. This was what brought the best out of her performances, she thought; the hot lights, the tumultuous applause, the audience drawing every single bit of talent out of her being. It was as if they pulled the best out of her with their enthusiasm and excitement. She was charged with an extra burst of energy that she couldn't explain.

She had already decided on her encore number. It was to be a softer number because she wanted to leave her audience in a reflective mood. She wanted to take all that charged emotion, prevalent throughout the entire performance, and turn it into an emotional moment. One of her favourite romantic melodies would do the job because it always brought about the best results. As she took the audience on a journey throughout her song, she played them like a well-tuned instrument. The only thing she regretted was that she couldn't see the faces of the audience as she weaved the melody. However, with her eyes closed, she could picture the impact of her performance on every one in earshot of her voice. It was a magical moment and one that would always remain in her memory. On the playing of the final note for the evening, she stepped from the stage exhausted, yet satisfied as she received yet another standing ovation.

She had met the audience with the intention of winning each and every one of them over. She had achieved that. She had given everything to the audience tonight, just as she did every other night. She knew that it was not only the music, nor the flamboyant clothing designs, nor the intricate lighting presentations or the fireworks that won their approval. It wasn't the video clips, or the lyrics of the songs that generated such a wonderful response from the crowd. It was all because she loved what she did; she loved the audience and was always excited to share her talent with them. She had dug deep tonight to draw out the very best she could offer.

Children, the deeper I dig the more excited I get. I am like the miner looking for gold or some other precious metal. He knows that with each incision into the face of the earth, with every stroke, with every excavation, with every blast of dynamite, he is getting closer to finding what he has been searching for. The excitement builds with each new detection. Every clue that has been backed up by his previous knowledge and experiences tells him when he is getting closer to his goal. The process of research and exploration though, is where the excitement really began.

It is like the joy that we have as we sit in front of a puzzle. Scattered pieces strewn across the floor or the table would appear to any onlooker as a mess, but in our mind's eye, we see the end product. We see the final picture and the completed work. So, with enthusiasm we embark on a journey that will take us to our desired end. We sometimes make a mistake here or there but we're never perturbed. We simply put the piece aside and pick up another one, until we finally choose the very last one and put it in its rightful place. As a child, we are not concerned with the fact that we misplace pieces repeatedly. Our excitement and enthusiasm overrides any delay in fulfiling the process. We simply pick up another piece or stop playing with the puzzle for a time and then come back later to try again.

This is so much like our lives. Life is not about hitting the mark each and every time. It is about having enough excitement to try and try again. It helps if we have a completed picture already in our mind. With that picture in place, we know that it's only a matter of time before we will put the right pieces in the right place.

Some call this picture the dream while others refer to it as a Life Goal. Another term is a Mission Statement. Whatever you wish to call it, and in whatever form you wish to place it, it really doesn't matter. The important thing is that you take time to write it down. As rough as you may write it, it really doesn't matter, but by committing it to paper you have stamped your mind with an image that is not easily forgotten or discarded.

There have been many times when after jotting down a goal onto a piece of paper I have stuffed it away for safekeeping in my wallet. From time to time, I have uncovered them again. To my utter surprise, I have found that many of the things that I noted down have been fulfiled.

I have long-term goals that take me from one or two years to five years. I even have some goals that take me to the end of my life. I also have short-term goals that could be as short as one day or into the next three months or even through to the end of the current year.

The thing about goals is that they give you the finished picture. I write them in the completed tense by using the words. *'I have …'* rather than the words *'I will …'*. This gives it greater power and gives me the completed picture rather than a picture that will one day be completed.

I attach a date of completion to the goal such as, *'I have …by the 25th December 2002'* and then I set about breaking that completed picture into smaller segments, just like the pieces that make up a puzzle. I simply dismantle the finished product at the beginning so that I will know how I can effectively build it.

Children, it is a bit like playing with Lego backwards. Included within a Lego packet is a plan for construction. On the packet, we have a picture of the finished product and inside the packet is a step by step plan to get us there. Whenever you have a goal, break it up into smaller steps. By doing each small step you will be able to arrive successfully at the completed goal.

I first attack a goal on a piece of paper before I physically start to work towards it. It doesn't take that long to do but what it does do is build belief and an increased excitement about the whole process of bringing a goal to pass.

The important thing about setting goals is to find out what you need to do on a daily basis. Once that is established, you can get to work immediately. Remember, it's what you do on a day to day basis that will make all the difference.

So, in summary, here is my four-step plan to having more excitement in your life than you know what to do with:

1. Establish a goal and write it down
2. Write down your daily plan of action
3. Share your goal with someone who will keep you accountable
4. Act on that plan, beginning now

This simple four-step process provides you with a working plan that will bring the goal to completion. I follow this plan when I write a book or when I start a new business plan. I use it with my exercise program. I apply it to my families' leisure activities. It works for my budget and cashflow projections.

Some plans are more elaborate than others are, but with this guide, I find that my excitement level rises because I now have a plan.

When is the best time to set new goals? Right now! If you already have the goal habit, sit down once a year and establish and review your yearly goals, to keep you on track for the coming year. It is also a good time to check if you're on track to fulfiling your long-term goals. Start each month by writing down the goals for the coming month and then on a Sunday afternoon or night write down what needs to be achieved in the up and coming week. A friend of mine promotes the use of 12-week goals. It places a greater urgency than having yearly goals, while giving you enough time to really make some significant inroads. This may work for you.

So, what is exciting about that? The knowledge that you're on track and on target for a fulfilled and successful life.

*I'm excited,
how about you?
Love Dad*

Learn from the past,
concentrate on today
and tomorrow
will take care
of itself.

THE 27TH LETTER

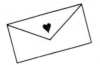

DoN't Be A cOpYcAt - SiMpLy TrAcE

To be called a copycat, as a child, was like having mud flung in your face. It was an insult. Every one of us wanted to be seen as someone who was unique in his or her own special way. We didn't want to be accused of using someone else's idea. We wanted to be original.

However, if the truth were known, there are very few completely original thoughts out there. What we often see are varied shades of an original idea that has been further improved or developed.

With any new invention or creative thought, you will find that its foundations are built upon the thoughts of those who have gone before. So, in order to live successfully you don't always have to come up with a completely original idea. In most cases, you can look at an already existing idea and search for ways to improve it.

So in encouraging you to trace, what do I mean? Let me explain it this way. Tracing involves taking an outline of some object or form. What you end up with is an exoskeleton. From that point on it is now your job to flesh the object out. It is your role to add the colour and the design. Based on the original foundation you can now build your own edifice. Is this proposing a breach of copyright? No. Is this promoting the idea of carrying around in our back pocket a piece of tracing paper and a pencil? No. I am encouraging you to keep your eyes and ears open. Open yourself up to discovering better ways to do something that someone may already be doing. Always be on the lookout for the better way; the innovative way. It has a lot to do with commonsense and a lot to do with being alert. Be a thinker and not just an acceptor of the status quo. Be thankful for the old ways but always stay supple in the hands of change. This is the principle that took the McDonalds business, owned by two brothers, to the point where Ray Kroc developed 4,000 outlets over the next twenty years. He took a good idea and made it so much better.

When a composer composes a new tune on an instrument, he or she has the same choice of notes that have been available to composers throughout the centuries. It is when he or she begins to place those same notes in a slightly different order, we have what we call an original song or melody.

Today, more than ever, there is an ever-increasing number of new things being created. However, every great new thought or design is built upon the resources of the past. As always, the past, the present and the future are inseparable. We must learn from the past, concentrate on today and tomorrow will take care of itself. Dreams are important, but it is what we have learnt from past experiences and what we are diligently undertaking today that will either thrust us towards or hold us back from the fulfilment of our dreams.

A great artist was once an unknown amateur. A successful writer, before receiving the accolades of his peers and the public, was stumbling over how to put two words together on a page. Before a sportsman, an entrepreneur, a diplomat, a surgeon or a philosopher achieved their status in society they were all novices. They were still tracing the footsteps of other great men or women in their chosen field, before they firmly placed their own two feet on solid rock.

Every time I read an autobiography, I find myself tracing over their life and taking it on board. I fill in the sketch in my mind as I see myself overcoming their difficulty. I see myself passing through their winning tape. I feel what they feel and taste their victory.

A tracer in fact draws upon others' experiences to enhance their own experience. This is why there is so much power in another person's story. We can take what applies to our own lives and apply it to our own. I do this every time when I read a book. I attack a book with pencil in hand and underline those points that strike to the heart of what I am looking for. I may not read every single word in the book because I am looking for the nuggets to be added to my own storehouse of ideas and inspiration. Those books that have a profound influence on my life, I take the time to type up my own summaries. What themes do I follow closely? Well, anything to do with success, the dream, reaching human potential and human development, anything that is of a motivational and inspirational nature, management, leadership, family, relationships and I love to read plenty of biographies and autobiographies.

I can trace back to major turning points in my life where I have been influenced by either a book or a tape that has come into my possession at the right time.

I have recently been reading the book *Simplicity* by Edward de Bono. He is a world renowned 'thinker' and in his book he proposes that in our world of great complexity we need to get back to finding simpler ways to doing things. He cites the fact that most of us don't even know how to use the basic operations of our microwave or video player ('tis true for me) and I know for sure that those who write the manuals for many of our appliances are not 'normal' human beings.

I know that from a personal standpoint I am always seeking to find a simpler way to explain complex subjects. It must be the teacher in me and I suppose it comes from my days of summarizing notes at school and college. I have always wanted to find out the guts of a subject. I would constantly cut away all the peripherals so that the only thing left standing was the skeleton. From that skeleton, I was then able to rebuild the subject more clearly in my mind.

Simple things enthrall me. I am constantly amazed at how

clever the simple paper clip is. Yet how many functions does it perform in an office on a daily basis? In addition, the Post it notes. Apparently, the inventor of these had failed to produce a suitable adhesive for another task but it proved suitable for his new idea. The Rubix cube made the designer by the same name a multi-millionaire. These are just a few simple ideas that have captured the imagination of millions. The fellow who decided to bottle the volcanic ash from Mt St Helen's volcano, a devastating disaster for many, sold them at $1 a bottle and was soon listed as a millionaire. I even have an eagle sitting on my desk designed out of compressed ash from that very same volcano.

In writing these letters to you my children, my goal is to learn to write clearly and simply so that people, even other children, can be encouraged, uplifted and guided. Jesus never used big words to explain his powerful truths. He was a carpenter and used everyday examples and stories to portray truth. He chose fishermen to be his companions. Sure, the educated soon joined his merry band such as Luke, the doctor and the Apostle Paul, but at the same time, Paul was a tentmaker and a tradesman. My trade is writing and my tool is my pen with no ink (otherwise known as a computer) and it's always exciting to see what can be squeezed out of a seemingly empty mind as it spills over and onto an empty page. One thing I have learnt: the more you give, the more you get to give again.

Simple minds using simple methods produce simply beautiful things. Whether it is a garden or a piece of prose. Whether it is a quilt or a painting. The Creator created you and me to be creative by using our gifts and our talents. To Him they are all as important and all as beautiful. The most important thing is that we use them for what they were created for; to bring joy to our creator, joy to others and joy to ourselves.

In all you do leave a trace element of love behind, always.
Love Dad

THE 28TH LETTER

ThInK aBoUt It

When you write an important letter, the first thing you need to do is think. All I have in front of me are the above three words, *'Think About It'*. I suppose that is why writing is at times such an incredible challenge. I want to write something significant: something that will impact your life and stay with you forever.

Some days are easier to write than others and in a recent letter that I sent to your grandmother I wrote the following, *"I've had another successful morning. At times when I sit in front of the computer it is like walking into a battlefield. The enemy; the empty page and the raging thoughts that bombard my mind, shout, 'You don't have one more original thought left do you? Why don't you just go back to bed and forget about it until another day.' I think someone once gave it the term 'Writers Bloc' but unbeknown to that little devilish thought, it is statements like that, that cause the writer's spirit inside me to rise up from within and declare, 'The Creator resides within this one and if He was able to create a whole world in six days then surely he can help this mortal create a mere book within forty-five.' Every paragraph completed is a skirmish won, every chapter finished a beachhead taken and when the last page is finally conquered, the war is over.*

One of the letters that I wrote to you recently came to my rescue today. As I referred to some notes by Emerson, I found that he came to the same conclusion. He writes, 'The experience of writing letters is one of the keys to the modus of inspiration. When

we have ceased for a long time to have any fullness of thoughts
that once made a diary of joy as well as a necessity, and have come
to believe that an image or a happy turn of expression is no longer
at our command, **in writing a letter to a friend we may find
that we rise to thought and to a cordial power of expression that
costs no effort** and it seems to us that this difficulty may be indef-
initely applied and resumed.'

I find great comfort from those who have gone before. I
suppose that is why we all need mentors. We all need to have somebody putting some positive input into our life, even if it is to give us
a shove along."

With every letter that I write to you, I am constantly
thinking about how I can creatively communicate truths that
have already been written by numerous authors throughout the
centuries. The message hasn't ever changed, only the delivery.
Because of our individual personality and style, a writer is able
to present a slightly different slant on a particular subject. My
role as a writer is to cause you to think and to not always
provide you with all the answers. For by the time you have
closed the pages of this book and returned it to your book-
shelf, you will have forgotten a vast majority of what I have
written. However, if I have achieved my goal of causing you to
think, to question, and to have a longing to learn, I have
succeeded. For it is in learning to ask the right questions that
will help you to obtain the right answers. This will in turn give
you great joy and satisfaction.

When I share a story, I am opening your mind up so that
you can begin to think. If I make you laugh, I am doing the
same. When I shock you with a fact, I have done it again. For
what is a book unless it opens peoples' minds? To succeed, they
must begin to think for themselves. Think about it!

Why is it that one book will stir one reader and yet leave
another cold? Why is it that I can pick up a book at one time
and find nothing but the taste of dirt in my mouth, whereas
at another time I extract diamonds from within the very same
pages? Think about it!

Why is it that two people can sit in the same seminar and

hear the same words, yet one will leave that seminar and achieve great success while the other will continue in their mediocrity? Think about it!

Why is it that one can live in great opulence while another lives in poverty, but the one who obtained wealth has never completed any formal education? Think about it!

Why is it that one who receives a high cash income can be poor whereas one who lives on a minimal wage can be rich? Think about it!

Why is it that one with small talent and great opposition can achieve so much while another with great talent and no opposition can achieve so little? Think about it!

Why is it that one soars and another falls by the way? Think about it!

What is the secret to long lasting success? Think about it!

What brings the greatest joy to one's life? Think about it!

What is success? Think about it!

Who is a winner? Think about it!

What separates a winner from a loser? Think about it!

How do I identify my strengths? Think about it!

How do I turn those strengths to my advantage? Think about it!

♥

Once there were two executives. Businessperson number one would leave messages for executive number two who would never return his telephone calls, or his e-mails. Number one would leave polite messages with number two's secretary and in all his communications would be courteous. Some time passed and still no telephone calls had been returned. Now both businessmen were very busy people but businessman number one always made it a priority to return phone calls within 24 to 48 hours. He thought that, in order to run professional organizations, others might consider to do the same. Finally, businessman number one leaves a message with the secretary of number two, *'Please ask number two why he never returns my phone calls or e-mails?'* The next day number one receives a call from number two. Number two is very angry, *'How dare you leave a message like that with my secretary'.* Number one smiles and says, *'Well the good thing is that you finally returned my call.'* The anger subsided, but the fact was; the question had achieved an answer.

In our own lives, there lives a number one and number two. Number one is the disciplined go-getter side of our personality, and number two is the side that is always looking for an easy way or for a rest along the way. It is always easier to slide to our number two side but by using the art of questioning we can guide ourselves over into our number one side more regularly. Number one gets the job done.

♥

Here's a few questions for you …

What will happen if I don't make that telephone call?
Or
What might happen if I do make that telephone call?

Where will I be in five years if I do what my mentor has instructed me to do?
Or
Where will I be in five years if I put my feet up and don't follow the basic ingredients that will get me where I want to be in five years?

As a writer I have to constantly ask myself; What if I don't sit down this morning for a few hours and type up another 1,000 words? Well I know exactly what answer I will receive. Another book that will help you my children and others, to achieve personal success, will not be completed.

Questions are powerful because they goad you on to think. Without questioning, we will simply float on down the stream like everybody else. The art of questioning pushes us over from our comfort zone and into the area where we are required to take action. Think about it!

One question that has spurred me on throughout the years is the question, *'What if?'* or in its expanded form, *'What if I do such and such?'* or *'What if I don't do such and such?'* It is one of those questions that makes you feel extremely uncomfortable. It causes you to take a serious look at your life. It is a challenge to your acceptance of any ounce of mediocrity left residing within your bones. It forces you to take stock of where you are, what you're doing and where you're going.

Questions that cause us to think about our life will prepare us in taking the next leap of faith and the next successful step. What questions should you be asking?

Think about it!
Love Dad

What if?

THE 29TH LETTER

It AiN't OvEr UnTiL ...

He crashed to the floor. The blow had come from nowhere, smashing against his lower jaw, jolting his whole body and penetrating deep beneath his defenses. Within seconds, after the perfect punch had connected with his face, he was flat on his back on the canvas. The count began. He didn't hear the first few numbers but by the time 5, 6, 7 were yelled, something on the inside of his chest stirred and the message was transmitted simultaneously to his body. He began to move. His mind didn't hear a thing but his body responded like a robot. All the training. All the discipline. All the input that he'd received from his coach these past months clicked in, just as an automatic pilot takes over the control of a plane in an instant. His instinctive desire to win declared that this night wasn't going to be his last. The fight wasn't over yet.

It was like a dream. He rolled to his side and could see himself lifting his bloodied face off the canvas. He could see his arms pushing down as though he was ready to do a set of pushups. He could see the beads of sweat drop from his brow, as if in slow motion, falling, falling, falling until they splashed and mingled with the blood, where he had just had his face.

He loved the hours of intense practice; working on the jab, the uppercut, the right cross, the left hook and the straight left. He loved the feel of his hands in the gloves. He took pride in the speed with which he could hit the speedball. In full swing, it was like magic, because the speedball would move so fast that it would at times seem to disappear completely.

He loved to hit, but like all fighters he hated being hit himself; but that was part and parcel of being a professional fighter. Cuts always healed, bruises always faded, but nothing could ever remove the incredible sensation of being the victor in a fight. There was nothing that could replace the sense of power which surged through his body when he connected with the face of an opponent so perfectly, and sent him sprawling across the ring until he fell like a stone. There was nothing sweeter than delivering a knockout. After the final bell was rung, there was no finer moment than to have your arm lifted up by the referee, in recognition of yet another win. Nothing could ever replace the sound of the applause as he was lifted up onto the shoulders of both his coach and his assistant to be paraded before the crowd.

At this very moment though, it had been his turn to be on the other end of a powerful uppercut. However, before the referee could reach number ten he had somehow regained consciousness and staggered to his feet. Although he could only see a blur before his eyes, he was ready to face another onslaught of punches from his opponent. Fortunately, before another punch could be thrown, the bell rang for the end of yet another round. It had already been a long fight and both fighters were tired from the incessant battering they had received from each other. They crawled back into their separate corners.

There was just enough time for the coach to shout more confidence into his ears as he wiped him down. He continued to repeat, *'Yer might have been down Tiger but yer not out.'* and *'It ain't over until it's over. He's getting just as tired as you are, so keep lookin' for his weakness. Keep searchin' and when he opens up, hit 'im with all yer might. Yer can do it Tiger. He's just keeping ya honest, that's all. Remember, it ain't over until it's over and I can tell yer now that it ain't over yet. So get out there and give 'im a hidin'"*

The bell rang, and inspired by his coaches powerful words

he pulled himself to his feet, recharged and reignited in spirit, even though his body was starting to feel the effects of the long fight. The blur had disappeared and the sharpness of eye had returned. He was set for the final kill. It was time to end this fight. It was time to finish off the opponent.

Both fighters dragged themselves around the ring for a few seconds sizing each other up. Sparring here and sparring there but not actually connecting. They knew that this was going to be the decider. They had both copped a fistful of punches; probably more than most humans would ever receive in a lifetime and the one who connected with just the right punch this time was going to win the fight.

Tiger, as his coach called him, delivered a few body blows, but he knew that they were ineffective. His opponent was built like solid steel. The only way that he could reach him was to get in a quick uppercut to the lower jaw, just like the one that had put him on the mat. Tiger landed a straight right into his opponent's face causing his nose to bleed. He then quickly followed this with a few more blows to the head before being held in a clinch. When the referee shouted at them to break up they both pushed each other away. His opponent took a wild swing but missed.

Avoiding the punch, Tiger slipped in a pool of sweat that lay on the floor. His opponent, seeing an opportunity to get him while he was vulnerable, leant over to bring down a powerful right cross. If it had connected it would have sent Tiger packing. However, as he leant over for a split second, he let his guard down and even while Tiger was starting to fall, he saw the opening. With the last vestige of strength left in his body Tiger brought his right fist around and struck straight up into the air with such speed that when it hit the opponent's jaw it dislodged his mouthguard and knocked his head back, as if a whip had just been cracked. While Tiger fell awkwardly to the ground his opponent staggered back, back, back until he hit the ropes and slid to the floor, like a slithering snake, unconscious. For a second the crowd gasped because both fighters had fallen and they thought they had just witnessed a double knockout, but as they continued to look on, Tiger pulled himself to his feet. The crowd went wild. He had won.

♥

'It ain't over until it's over.' Very wise words, I must say. Words that I would like to leave to you my children. When your back is up against the wall, when there doesn't seem to be any way out and no possible means of escape, when the pressure is on and when the chips are down, always remember that *'it ain't over until it's over.'* While ever there is breath in your body and while ever there is hope in your heart, hold on. You will find a way through, if not under, then over or even around whatever you are facing at the time. There will always be a way and you will always find it if you simply decide that you will.

Problems have been given to us in our lifetime so that we can find solutions. Ask any inventor. They make their livelihood out of solving problems. Problems are the stuff that make us strong and resilient. Without challenges, we would grow weak and insipid. It is only as pressure is put on a muscle that it develops strength. Problems are the gymnasium in which we can get our best workout as human beings. Those who avoid such exercise will always be weak in character. Those who accept the fact that life will always present us with challenges to overcome will grow strong in both character and integrity.

There are many who will sit on the sidelines, but few who will dare to step onto the canvas and into the midst of the battle. It is in the ring where one is bloodied and bruised, but it is in the ring where the victor is applauded. I have never seen those out in the crowd ever being applauded, have you? No, it is the participator. The contender for the crown is placed in a position where he or she can either win or lose, succeed or fail. Those who stay outside the ring will never get the chance to experience either. They live their lives in mediocrity with no applause and with no shame, just plain ordinary. They will never win, they will never fail and therefore they will never be.

As for me, I would rather venture into the ring where if I fail, I fail with dignity and if I succeed, I succeed with humility. At least at the end of my days I will be able to say that throughout my life my creed was, *'It ain't over until it's over.'*

Yet when I breathe my final breath you will be able to proudly say of me, *'He fought. He won. It is now over.'*

Champions together
Love Dad

*Having an open
mind will ward off
the onset of
mental rigor mortis
or
vision arthritis.*

THE 30TH LETTER

DoN't BlInK

Whenever we travel throughout this great country, there are times when we will pass through a small country town. Before we reach it I often say to you, *'Don't blink, because you might miss it.'*

In this my last letter, I want to leave you with a poem rather than a letter. Our life is very much like those country towns. Before you know it, children have become adults in the blink of an eye. Make every moment count and treat every day as a precious gift. For …

♥

Years have passed
In the blink of an eye
In a moment of time
Years have passed by

Throw caution to the wind
It's time to take stock
Turn back the hand
And look at the clock

Just for a minute
Stop and consider

How a second gave birth
To a minute, an hour
Developed the day
That a year has devoured

Seasons have come
Seasons have gone
Morning, noon
Night and dawn

What has one learnt
As he peers through the years?

That time used unwisely
And spent without thought
Will make you a pauper
And leave you with naught

But time that's well spent
Will stitch upon stitch
Weave memories and dreams
That will make your life rich.

♥

I love you, with every single piece of daddy's heart.
Dad

AbOuT tHe AuThOr

Peter Sinclair is a student of success and an entrepreneur, whose vision is to use both entertainment and education to help others reach their full potential. The driving force of his life and his work is to lift people. He is renowned and respected as a dynamic writer, speaker, composer and performer. His signature, at many of his major speaking engagements, is a grand piano, which he skillfully uses to demonstrate to both men and women, how they can live successful lives. He is married to Shelley and is the proud father of three children. Peter and his family reside on the Gold Coast in Australia and love to impart wisdom into the lives of people from all around the world.